The Apocalyptic Vision
A Thematic Exploration of Postwar German Literature

Alan Frank Keele

 studia humanitatis

Publisher and distributor
    José Porrúa Turanzas, S.A.
    Cea Bermúdez, 10 - Madrid-3
    España

Distributor for U.S.A.
    Studia Humanitatis
    1383 Kersey Lane
    Potomac, Maryland 20854

© Alan Frank Keele 1983
Library of Congress Catalog Card Number 82-082404
International Standard Book Number 0-935568-40-9

Printed in the United States of America
Impreso en Los Estados Unidos

Cea Bermúdez, 10 - Madrid-3
Ediciones José Porrúa Turanzas, S.A.

The Apocalyptic Vision:
A Thematic Exploration of Postwar German Literature

José Porrúa Turanzas, S.A.
EDICIONES

Director General:
JOSÉ PORRÚA VENERO

Sub-Director General:
ENRIQUE PORRÚA VENERO

Director:
CONSTANTINO GARCÍA GARVÍA

Asesor literario:
BRUNO M. DAMIANI

studia humanitatis

Directed by
BRUNO M. DAMIANI
The Catholic University of America

ADVISORY BOARD

JUAN BAUTISTA AVALLE-ARCE
University of North Carolina

THEODORE BEARDSLEY
The Hispanic Society of America

GIOVANNI MARIA BERTINI
Università di Torino

HEINRICH BIHLER
Universität Göttingen

HAROLD CANNON
National Endowment for the Humanities

DANTE DELLA TERZA
Harvard University

FRÉDÉRIC DELOFFRE
Université de Paris-Sorbonne

O. B. HARDISON
The Folger Shakespeare Library

HANS FLASCHE
Universität Hamburg

ROBERT J. DIPIETRO
University of Delaware

GIOVANNI FALLANI
Musei Vaticani

JOHN E. KELLER
University of Kentucky

RICHARD KINKADE
University of Arizona

JUAN M. LOPE BLANCH
Universidad Nacional Autónoma de México

LELAND R. PHELPS
Duke University

MARTÍN DE RIQUER
Real Academia Española

JOSEPH SILVERMAN
University of California (Santa Cruz)

To Theodore and Yetta Ziolkowski, "den Zaubermeistern."

Contents

Part One
The Origins and Nature of the Apocalyptic Vision

CHAPTER ONE   "... through a (dark) glass clearly": Magic Spectacles and the Motif of the Mimetic Mantic in Postwar German Literature   3

CHAPTER TWO   The Symbolical Limp and the Secular Postwar Seer   35

Part Two
The Apocalyptic View of Certain Contemporary Phenomena

CHAPTER THREE   The Terrible Toys: A View from Postwar German Literature at the Process of Play-Time Psychological Pre-Conditioning for Dictatorship, War and Holocaust   55

CHAPTER FOUR   Reptiles and Robots: Minacious Machinery and its Automaton-Slaves   93

CHAPTER FIVE   Ethics in Embryo: Abortion and the Problem of Morality in Postwar German Literature   107

Index   127

Preface

Even a rather small handbook of German literary authors of the three decades from 1945 to 1975 lists over 350 names and several thousand stories, plays, novels, essays and volumes of poetry.[1] Until the ravages of time and continued literary scholarship have eroded away less-durable portions of that mass and exposed any monumental peaks contained within, it may be impossible for critics to attempt anything like a definitive study of postwar German literature. Still, there are cracks and crevices in the landscape, points of entry into the *terra incognita*, so to speak, including those test holes bored and trenches hacked out by scholars interested in individual authors, works and subjects. This book is an attempt to descend into such fissures and to follow five thematic red threads through the postwar German literary labyrinth.

On the spoor of magical eyeglasses, limping prophets,

---

[1] Elisabeth Endres, *Autorenlexikon der deutschen Gegenwartsliteratur 1945–1975* (Frankfurt: Fischer, 1975).

martial toys, games and sports, powerful engines, robots and hydrogen bombs, abortion, suicide, genocide and the death of God, this book explores the works of such authors as (Nobel-laureate) Heinrich Böll, Wolfgang Borchert, Günter Grass, Siegfried Lenz, Paul Schallück and Martin Walser. At the end of the expedition, the entire landmass will certainly not have been thoroughly mapped. But the reader will have encountered some unusual formations and unexpected vistas—not all *atypical* of the entire landscape, it is hoped—and be tempted to undertake future, perhaps more profitable forays into this fascinating terrain.

Though no doubt imperfectly, this book attempts to bridge the gap between scholarly specialists in *Germanistik* and general, well-educated American readers.[2] I undertook this quixotic task because postwar German literature itself is frankly *engagé*; consequently, a kind of literary criticism *engagé* suggested itself. I am persuaded (in no small part by the postwar German authors themselves) that literature *and* literary scholarship—in fact, all scholarship—must not become mere "calligraphy" but must attempt, insofar as possible, to meet contemporary problems head-on. Whether actual scholarly objectivity must be sacrificed to achieve such a goal, I cannot say: certainly I have not consciously sacrificed any. At the very least, I hope it cannot be said that I appear bored by postwar German literature. And if my readers can say the same about themselves when they have finished this small work, I will be pleased.

Portions of chapters two and four appeared in my monograph *Paul Schallück and the Postwar German Don Quixote: A Case-History Prolegomenon to the Literature of the Federal Republic*

---

[2] For example, though quotations from German works are in German, I have tried to summarize their content nearby in the English text itself. One does not, I believe, need to know German to understand this book.

(Bern: Lang, 1976). A much shorter version of chapter three, parts of chapter one, and an earlier version of chapter five appeared in *Soundings, An Interdisciplinary Journal* and in *The Germanic Review*, respectively.[3]

Special thanks is due James K. Lyon, my colleagues Marvin Folsom and George Tate, as well as Deans Garold Davis and Richard Cracroft of the College of Humanities, Brigham Young University, for intellectual, moral and financial support leading to the completion of this project.

Provo, Utah
May, 1982

---

[3] *Soundings*, Vol. LXV, No. 2, pp. 146–167; *The Germanic Review*, Vol. LVII, No. 2, pp. 49–59 and Vol. LI, No. 3, pp. 229–241. (All sections reprinted by permission.)

Part One
The Origins and Nature of the Apocalyptic Vision

CHAPTER ONE

" . . . through a (dark) glass clearly": Magic Spectacles and the Motif of the Mimetic Mantic in Postwar German Literature

I

One of the most seminal documents of postwar German literature—even today probably still the best-known and most-often performed work of that era—is Wolfgang Borchert's epoch-making *Hörspiel* "Draussen vor der Tür" (1947). And what person who is familiar with it does not, at the very mention of Borchert's play, immediately call to mind the grotesque *Gasmaskenbrille* of Beckmann, its pathetic protagonist? These eyeglasses, in fact, with the possible exception of Beckmann's limp, are the most pervasive 'leitmotif' of the entire work, and our attention is drawn to them by practically every character in practically every scene.

The young girl, for example, who fishes Beckmann out of the river after his unsuccessful suicide attempt, comments on these before anything else:

> MÄDCHEN: So, nun will ich mir erstmal den geangelten Fisch unter der Lampe ansehen. Nanu—(sie lacht) aber sagen Sie um Himmels willen, was soll denn dies hier sein?
> BECKMANN: Das? Das ist meine Brille. Ja. Sie lachen. Das ist meine Brille. Leider.
> MÄDCHEN: Das nennen Sie Brille? Ich glaube, Sie sind mit Absicht komisch.

BECKMANN: Ja, meine Brille. Sie haben recht: vielleicht sieht sie ein bisschen komisch aus. Mit diesen grauen Blechrändern um das Glas. Und dann diese grauen Bänder, die man um die Ohren machen muss. Und dieses graue Band quer über die Nase! Man kriegt so ein graues Uniformgesicht davon. So ein blechernes Robotergesicht. So ein Gasmaskengesicht. Aber es ist ja auch eine Gasmaskenbrille.
MÄDCHEN: Gasmaskenbrille?
BECKMANN: Gasmaskenbrille. Die gab es für die Soldaten, die eine Brille trugen. Damit sie auch unter der Gasmaske was sehen konnten.[1]

It is also the girl who first playfully suggests that these ugly spectacles may have a certain power over Beckmann and his outlook: "Ich glaube, Sie machen nur so einen trostlosen Eindruck, weil Sie immer durch diese grauenhafte Gasmaskenbrille sehen müssen." She, too, first suggests that they may be the exterior manifestation of or symbol for an interior condition: "Ich glaube, Sie tragen auch innerlich so eine Gasmaskenbrille Sie behelfsmässiger Fisch."[2]

Like the girl, the director of a cabaret also immediately notices Beckmann's spectacles and asks him why he doesn't discard them. Beckmann replies "Ich bin glücklich, dass ich wenigstens diese habe. Das ist meine Rettung. Es gibt doch sonst keine Rettung—keine Brillen, meine ich."[3] The cabaret director boasts that *he* has three pairs of first-class horn-rimmed glasses—clearly the civilian counterpole to Beckmann's—"eine gelbe zum Arbeiten. Eine unauffällige zum Ausgehen. Und eine abends für die Bühne, verstehen Sie, eine schwarze, schwere Hornbrille."[4] When Beckmann asks if he might give him one, the director replies: "Wo denken Sie hin, mein bester Mann? Von meinen paar Brillen kann ich keine einzige entbehren. Meine ganzen Einfälle, meine Wir-

---

[1] Wolfgang Borchert, *Das Gesamtwerk* (Hamburg: Rowohlt, 1949), p. 112.
[2] Ibid., p. 114.
[3] Ibid., p. 131.
[4] Ibid.

kung, meine Stimmungen sind von ihnen abhängig." "Ja, das ist es eben," says Beckmann sadly, "meine auch."[5]

With his (exterior and interior) glasses, clearly representative of those higher, visionary optics gained by his experience in war, Beckmann is, in the literal sense of the term, a *'Seher'*, a seer whose 'X-ray vision' allows (or rather forces) him to strip away facades and *see* deeply into the essence of things. To his old colonel, for example (whose wife also immediately notices the glasses: "Vater, sag ihm doch, er soll die Brille abnehmen. Mich friert, wenn ich das sehe."), before launching into a description of his recurring vision of the dead, he makes the significant statement: "ich sehe ohne Brille alles verschwommen. Aber so kann ich alles *erkennen*."[6]

No camouflage or smoke screen, not even linguistic ones, can be used to hide the truth from this seer, hence he insists, for example, that the word 'responsibility' be taken as literally and as seriously as the fate of those millions in his nightmare:

OBERST: Was wollen Sie denn von mir?
BECKMANN: Ich bringe sie Ihnen zurück.
OBERST: Wen?
BECKMANN (beinah naiv): Die Verantwortung. Ich bringe Ihnen die Verantwortung zurück. Haben Sie das ganz vergessen, Herr Oberst? Den 14. Februar? Bei Gorodok. Es waren 42 Grad Kälte . . . dann sagten Sie: Unteroffizier Beckmann, ich übergebe Ihnen die Verantwortung für die zwanzig Mann . . . und als wir wieder in der Stellung waren, da fehlten elf Mann. Und ich hatte die Verantwortung.
OBERST: Aber mein lieber Beckmann, Sie erregen sich unnötig. So war es doch nicht gemeint.
BECKMANN (ohne Erregung, aber ungeheuer ernsthaft): Doch. Doch, Herr Oberst. So muss das gemeint sein. Verantwortung ist doch nicht nur ein Wort, eine chemische Formel, nach der helles Menschenfleisch in dunkle Erde verwandelt wird.

---

[5] *Ibid.*, p. 132.
[6] *Ibid.*, p. 120.

Man kann doch Menschen nicht für ein leeres Wort sterben lassen....[7]

To Beckmann, who sees the essence of all things clearly through his glasses (though his *alter ego* 'der Andere' accuses *him* of distorted vision), all the 'normal' people, including his 'verbal murderers' the colonel, the cabaret director and Frau Kramer, are unseeing human robots or marionettes, never 'en*vision*ing' through their 'uniform, apathetic, horrible *visages*' the deadly consequences of their words and deeds:

DER ANDERE: Du träumst, Beckmann, wach auf.
BECKMANN: Träum ich? Seh ich alles verzerrt durch diese elende Gasmaskenbrille? Sind alles Marionetten? Groteske, karikierte Menschenmarionetten?... Soll ich leben bleiben? Soll ich weiterhumpeln auf der Strasse? Neben den anderen? Sie haben alle dieselben gleichen gleichgültigen entsetzlichen *Visagen*. Und sie reden alle so unendlich viel.... Sie haben uns verraten. So furchtbar verraten. Wie wir noch ganz klein waren, da haben sie Krieg gemacht. Und als wir grösser waren, da haben sie vom Krieg erzählt. Begeistert. Immer waren sie begeistert. Und als wir dann noch grösser waren, da haben sie sich auch für uns einen Krieg ausgedacht. Und dann haben sie uns dann hingeschickt. Und sie waren begeistert. Immer waren sie begeistert. Und keiner hat uns gesagt, wo wir hingingen. Keiner hat uns gesagt, ihr geht in die Hölle. Oh nein, keiner. Sie haben Marschmusik gemacht und Langemarckfeiern und Kriegsgerichte und Aufmarschpläne. Und Heldengesänge und Blutorden.... Und sie haben uns nichts gesagt. Nur—Macht's gut, Jungens! haben sie gesagt.... So haben sie uns verraten. So furchtbar verraten. Und jetzt sitzen sie hinter ihren Türen. Herr Studienrat, Herr Direktor, Herr Gerichtsrat, Herr Oberarzt. Jetzt hat uns keiner hingeschickt. Nein, keiner.... Und jetzt gehen sie an ihrem Mord vorbei, einfach vorbei.[8]

The burden of Beckmann's visionary optics—actually

---

[7] *Ibid.*, p. 125f.
[8] *Ibid.*, p. 157f. (Emphasis added, here and throughout the book.)

the old disparity between *Sein* and *Schein*—which has already once driven him to attempt suicide, is probably more than he can bear, and though he insists that the eyeglasses are his salvation, there can be little hope for a seer like him. In Martin Walser's novel of a decade later, *Ehen in Phillipsburg* (1957) a likewise limping, perspicacious Beckmann-figure named Berthold Klaff also cannot continue to live with the *onus* of what he sees under the facades of life. Shortly before his suicide he visits his young neighbor, the radio and television critic Hans Beumann:

> Es klopfte. . . . Ein junger Mann stand unter der Tür, ein paar Jahre älter als Hans, ein schwerer Körper, rund, ohne jede Gliederung, eine wüste Windjacke hing über allem, kein Hals, ein riesiger Kopf direkt auf den hochwölbenden Schultern, die farblosen Haare lagen überall auf, wuchsen schon wieder aufwärts, und *das Gesicht hörte nirgends auf*.[9] Diese Körpermasse war nicht Wohlgenährtheit. Hans sprang auf. Der andere trat näher. Mit ungleichen Schritten. Hob er den rechten Fuss, so machte das ihm so viel Mühe, dass der Oberkörper nach vorne knickte. Also Herr Klaff. Da sagte er es auch schon: 'Berthold Klaff.' Hans nannte seinen Namen und räumte die Bücher vom Stuhl, verteilte sie aber so auf die anderen, dass der Besucher nicht mehr *erkennen* sollte, mit welcher Art Lektüre Hans die Nacht hinbrachte. *Klaffs Augen zeichneten*, bevor sie einen Augenblick in Hans' Gesicht Ruhe fanden, *Blitzlinien durchs Zimmer. Sie fuhren herum wie der Strahl eines Leuchtturmscheinwerfers*, der immer hastiger nach einem Ertrinkenden sucht, der in der Nähe des Turms mit den Wellen kämpft. Es war schwer, Berthold Klaff gegenüberzusitzen. Hans tat, als schmerze ihn einer seiner Handrücken, als müsse er *mit mikroskopischen Augen* nach der Ursache des Schmerzes forschen.[10]

If Hans' vision is *micro*scopic, Klaff's visual lightning bolts are *macro*- or *tele*scopic, for they plumb those depths of hypocrisy and self-deceit in Phillipsburg society in which Hans is in danger of drowning. And at first the seer is able to

---

[9] The term *Gesicht* of course, like *Visagen* in the passage immediately before, can imply 'vision' as well as 'face.'
[10] Martin Walser, *Ehen in Phillipsburg* (Reinbek: rororo, 1963), p. 61.

help Hans, especially after Hans hears Klaff's powerful *Hörspiel*. Hans is so excited by his new mentor's insights that he writes a glowing review of the *Hörspiel* for his employer's radio magazine, and he even suggests hiring Klaff as a critic. But his employer, much like the cabaret director in "Draussen vor der Tür" (which Klaff's *Hörspiel* itself greatly resembles), rejects the idea out of hand, telling Hans that Klaff's insights are so uncompromisingly stark that they would be bad for business. Consequently, Hans denies the truth of Klaff's visions and gradually adopts his employer's view as his own.

Abandoned by his wife, rejected by Hans, and having been fired from his previous job because his boss felt uncomfortable about Klaff constantly 'looking right through him,'[11] the seer commits suicide. Nevertheless, even after his death, and though Hans does not follow his advice, for Hans Beumann Klaff represents the only truly ethical counterweight in all of Phillipsburg society. Even in death he serves as Hans' conscience. His books still exist, the almost completely corrupted Beumann later laments, "selbst wenn er sie verbrannte, Klaff hatte gelebt."[12]

The seer Klaff, even in death, like Beckmann and other postwar wearers of exterior or interior *Gasmaskenbrillen* we shall yet encounter, is a walking anachronism, wrenched from the stream of 'normal time' by his visions beneath the facades. In Heinrich Böll's *Billard um halb zehn* (1959) there are two such timeless prods to the consciences of the wicked 'buffalos' inhabiting the novel, the 'lamb' Ferdi who, like Klaff, is dead; and Alfred Schrella, mysterious but very much alive and who, when he first finally appears in the novel "blickte über die

---

[11] *Ibid.*, p. 99.
[12] *Ibid.*, p. 221.

Brillengläser hinweg Nettlinger an."[13] Nettlinger, readers of Böll's novel will recall, was the Hitler-youth crony of Ben Wackes, that infamous coach with a whip made of barbed wire who had killed many of the 'lambs' and driven Schrella into exile. Now an important government official, Nettlinger magnanimously drives to the jail to free Alfred Schrella who had been arrested at the German border upon his return from England. Though the war has been over for more than a decade, his name remained on the wanted-list where it was placed during the Third Reich by none other than Nettlinger himself.

"Das Auto hielt vor einer Verkehrsampel," the story continues: "Schrella nahm seine Brille ab, wischte sie mit seinem Taschentuch und neigte sich nahe ans Fenster. 'Es muss dir doch merkwürdig vorkommen,' sagte Nettlinger, 'nach so langer Zeit und unter solchen Umständen wieder in Deutschland zu sein; du wirst es nicht wieder*erkennen*.' " "Ich *erkenne* es sogar wieder . . ." replies Schrella, picking up on that significant verb before continuing to paint a metaphorical picture of *Wirtschaftswunder*-Germany:

> ungefähr, wie man eine Frau wieder*erkennt,* die man als Mädchen geliebt hat und zwanzig Jahre später wiedersieht; nun, sie ist ein bisschen fett geworden; talgige Drüsen; offenbar hat sie einen nicht nur reichen, sondern auch fleissigen Mann geheiratet; Villa am Stadtrand, Auto, Ringe an den Fingern, die frühere Liebe wird unter solchen Umständen unvermeidlicherweise zu Ironie.[14]

This image of Germany's lost virtue seems distorted to Nettlinger and he questions Schrella's eyesight: " 'Natürlich sind solche Bilder ziemlich schief', sagte Nettlinger. . . . 'Es scheint mir auch zweifelhaft, ob deine *Optik* die richtige ist: vierundzwanzig Stunden erst im Lande, davon dreiundzwanzig im

---

[13] Heinrich Böll, *Billard um halb zehn* (Munich: Knaur, 1963), p. 146.
[14] *Ibid.*, p. 148.

Gefängnis.' " "Wenn du dreitausend [solche Bilder] hättest," the seer Schrella replies, "*sähst* du vielleicht ein Zipfelchen von der Wahrheit." Like Klaff, but especially like Beckmann, Schrella is a limping, visionary literalist, reacting even to such 'insignificant' things as words. He tells Nettlinger that he has spent a great deal of time in jail in the last 23 years—in Holland and in England—for that very reason:

> Ich bedrohte einen holländischen Politiker, weil er gesagt hatte, man müsste alle Deutschen umbringen, einen sehr beliebten Politiker; dann liessen die Deutschen mich frei, als sie Holland besetzten, und glaubten, ich sei eine Art Märtyrer für Deutschland, fanden aber dann meinen Namen auf der Fahndungsliste, und ich floh vor ihrer Liebe nach England; dort bedrohte ich einen englischen Politiker, weil er sagte, man müsste alle Deutschen umbringen, nur ihre Kunstwerke retten, einen sehr beliebten Politiker. . . .[15]

When he focuses his vision on a current German politician, a certain Kretz, "ein Star der Opposition," Schrella says: "Wenn der eine Hoffnung ist, möchte ich wissen, was eine Verzweiflung sein könnte . . . ich glaube, wenn ich mal jemand umbringen würde, dann ihn. *Seid ihr denn alle blind?*"[16]

Though the parallels are many and quite obvious, in at least one significant way Schrella differs from Klaff and Beckmann: He is not a suicide but a survivor. His visions may be uncomfortable, but he bears them stoically, or better, realistically. He makes political use of his insights, for example, not only to threaten 'buffalos' directly, but to help create a new circle of like-minded 'lambs' dedicated to identifying and opposing them in many other nonviolent ways.

The genesis of this significant—life affirming—variation

---
[15] *Ibid.*, p. 149.
[16] *Ibid.*, p. 232.

on the theme of the suicidal seer can be traced, I believe, to Siegfried Lenz' early tale "Die Nacht im Hotel" (1949). In this story a man named Schwamm tries to find an accommodation late at night in a crowded city and is forced to share a room with a stranger who, he is informed by the desk clerk, is already asleep. Reluctantly Schwamm enters the room and reaches for the light switch only to hear a voice say: "Halt! Bitte machen Sie kein Licht. Sie würden mir einen Gefallen tun, wenn Sie das Zimmer dunkel liessen." Verbally, the stranger directs Schwamm through the pitch-dark room to his bed, steering him around several obstacles:

> Stolpern Sie nicht über meine Krücken, und seien Sie vorsichtig, dass Sie nicht über meinen Koffer fallen, der ungefähr in der Mitte des Zimmers steht. Ich werde Sie sicher zu Ihrem Bett dirigieren: Gehen Sie drei Schritte an der Wand entlang, und dann wenden Sie sich nach links, und wenn Sie wiederum drei Schritte getan haben, werden Sie den Bettpfosten berühren können.[17]

Schwamm finds his bed, gets in and introduces himself to the stranger, whereupon, in the dark, a brief conversation ensues, the crux of which is that Schwamm has come to the city because of his son, a boy who is "äusserst sensibel, mimosenhaft," who "reagiert bereits, wenn ein Schatten auf ihn fällt," and who has "eine Glasseele und darum ist er bedroht." The boy, it seems, must pass a railroad crossing on his way to school and, though he always waves at the people in the train, no one ever waves back. He has become so despondent that his parents are greatly concerned. The stranger, listening quietly in bed, at most asking a few rather bizarre, disjointed questions ("Wollen Sie in der Stadt Selbstmord begehen?") now suddenly becomes very interested in the story and appears to grasp the rest of it without being told: "Und Sie, Herr Schwamm," he interjects, "wollen nun das

---

[17] Siegfried Lenz, *Erzählungen* (Stuttgart: Deutscher Bücherbund, 1970), p. 150 ff.

Elend Ihres Jungen aufsaugen [pun obviously intended], indem Sie morgen den Frühzug nehmen, um dem Kleinen zu winken?" Though it could be argued at this point in the narrative that the stranger does not want the light turned on and is able to direct Schwamm to his bed simply because his eyes had adjusted to the darkness; or that any halfway imaginative person could have guessed the plan to wave from the train, what occurs next *cannot* be explained realistically: "Sie fahren nach Kurzbach, nicht wahr?" the stranger asks, and Schwamm confirms it, though there is no reference at all anywhere else in the story to his hometown. In light of this statement, the previous utterances and actions of the mysterious stranger also take on mantic overtones, all of which suggest that Schwamm is sharing a room with a Beckmannesque limping seer, a visionary literalist (hence the pun on the name Schwamm, for example) who has come to the city to commit suicide because he, too, a *Doppelgänger* of the boy, has a 'glass soul'—an exact reification of the metaphor 'interior *Gasmaskenbrille.*' As with Beckmann and Klaff, these extraordinary gifts of perception endanger both the stranger and the boy. Behind the simple outward 'fact' that no one waves from the train, for example, these seers perceive a profoundly life-threatening coldness and inhumanity.

When Schwamm awakens alone in the room next morning, he realizes that he has overslept and has missed the morning train. Dejectedly he returns home on the afternoon one, only to be surprised by his son: "Sein Junge öffnete ihm die Tür, glücklich, ausser sich vor Freude. Er warf sich ihm entgegen und hämmerte mit den Fäusten gegen seinen Schenkel und rief: 'Einer hat gewinkt, einer hat ganz lange gewinkt!'" "Mit einer Krücke?" asks Schwamm, beginning to sense a connection to the stranger in the hotel room. "Ja, mit einem Stock," replies the boy. "Und zuletzt hat er sein Taschentuch an den Stock gebunden und es so lange aus dem

Fenster gehalten, bis ich es nicht mehr sehen konnte." Lenz' limping seer, suddenly forsaking his suicidal plans to help a likewise endangered kindred spirit, demonstrates that the burden of his visionary optics is not only life threatening, as in the case of Beckmann and Klaff, it can be life affirming and even life saving as well.

II

Having become increasingly attentive through Borchert, Walser, Böll and Lenz to such individually insignificant words as *blind, erkennen, Blitzlinien, Gesicht, mikroskopisch, Visagen, sehen, Glasseele* and *Optik,* as well as to such seemingly innocent fictional or dramatic props as a pair of spectacles, we can now tentatively posit the existence, from Borchert on,[18] of what appears to be a fairly common and fairly simple postwar German literary device, the recognition of which, however, seems quite useful—on occasion—to the exegetical process. And though there are undoubtedly more works dealing with this or related motifs (any further examples encountered by the reader will, it is hoped, tend to confirm the general pattern) one such work, Günter Grass' *Hundejahre* (1963) demands to be discussed at greater length.

In this novel we read of a new kind of toy being placed on

---

[18] A simple attempt to trace the history of eyeglasses in literature further backward or outward from postwar Germany would, I fear (even allowing for extraordinary good luck in the process of serendipity, since it appears that no one has yet compiled a compendium of spectacle wearers in world literature) only lead into a morass of random and hardly catalogueable occurrences. Some, of course, like Harry Haller in Hermann Hesse's *Steppenwolf* (Frankfurt: Suhrkamp, 1972) seem strikingly similar to the stock postwar motif. Thus we learn from the narrator that Haller's "unvergesslicher und furchtbarer *Blick*" has the power to cut immediately to the heart of matters (p. 13). Also premonitory of Borchert, it is a *Mädchen* in the role of savior who later says to the suicidal, limping Steppenwolf: "Komm, wische dir erst die *Brille* ab, du kannst ja gar nicht sehen" (p. 96).

the market around Christmas time in 1955 by a certain Brauxel & Co. And though they are never openly advertised for sale, are not available in toy shops, department stores or catalogues, and are not even given a name by the mysterious manufacturer, almost 1.5 million are sold within a few months. Stranger yet, these remarkably successful toys are nothing more than ordinary eyeglasses with cheap plastic frames and simple flat glass lenses, sold from cardboard boxes by vendors standing unobtrusively between booths at carnivals or near playgrounds and schools. But because of a secret patented ingredient in the glass, these 'Wunderbrillen,' 'Erkennungsbrillen,' 'Erkenntnisbrillen,' 'Vatererkennungsbrillen' or 'Muttererkennungsbrillen' as they are variously known among the young people who buy them, have the magical power to reveal to anyone between the ages of seven and twenty-one the hidden deeds and misdeeds, especially in war, of his or her parents:

> Die Wunderbrille zeigt jugendlichen Brillenträgern die Vergangenheit der Eltern in wechselnden Bildern, oft genug und bei einiger Geduld in chronologischer Folge. Episoden, die aus diesen oder jenen Gründen den heranwachsenden Kindern verschwiegen wurden, werden greifbar deutlich. . . . Immerhin—und erstaunlicherweise—kann man vermuten, dass nicht erschreckend viele erotische Geheimnisse gelüftet werden—es bleibt bei den üblichen Seitensprüngen—vielmehr wiederholen sich im doppelten Rund der Vatererkennungsbrillen Gewalttaten, verübt geduldet veranlasst vor elf zwölf dreizehn Jahren: Mord, oft hundertfacher. Beihilfe zum. Zigarettenrauchen und zusehen, während. Bewährte dekorierte umjubelte Mörder . . . mit Mördern an einem Tisch, im gleichen Boot, Bett und Kasino. Trinksprüche, Einsatzbefehle. Aktenvermerke. Stempel anhauchen. Manchmal sind es nur Unterschriften. . . . Viele Wege führen zum. . . . Jeder Vater hat wenigstens einen zu verbergen. Viele bleiben so gut wie ungeschehen, verschüttet verhängt eingemietet, bis im elften Nachkriegsjahr die Wunderbrillen auf den Markt kommen und Täter zur Schau stellen.[19]

---

[19] Günter Grass, *Hundejahre* (Hamburg: rororo, 1968), p. 407 f.

Instantly we recognize our motif. Even the terms *Erkennungs-* or *Erkenntnisbrille* evoke significant passages from Borchert, Walser and Böll: "Aber so kann ich alles *erkennen* ...," " ... dass der Besucher nicht mehr *erkennen* sollte ... " and "Ich *erkenne* es sogar wieder ... " Hidden murders and murderers are revealed in a vision as horrible as that of Beckmann's nightmare. Here, too—considerably expanded—are the familiar ideas from Lenz and Böll of a community of seers and of their higher vision as a source of (life-affirming) political action: Now, rather than merely symbolizing the unique optical perspectives brought home from the war by a few lonely, limping, suicidal seers, the enterprising Brauxel's spectacles actually impart that same perspective to hundreds of thousands who were themselves too young to experience the war. By the simple act of donning his eyeglasses these young people immediately see the world as Beckmann, Klaff, Schrella and The Man in the Hotel saw it.

Of course such an undertaking is fraught with risks and may not succeed. There may be some more like Klaff and Beckmann among those young eyeglass purchasers as well as those like Schrella and The Man in the Hotel. In fact, some young spectacle wearers do run away from home, we read, and a few commit suicide, at the news of which Brauxel & Co. immediately curtail their sales program. Yet another problem —perhaps even more serious—is that most purchasers of the glasses choose to ignore the vision it provides for them and continue with business as usual. In their obvious attempt to make seers of the nation's youth, then, Brauxel & Co. have achieved only very limited success. But the fact that they would attempt this at all is significant and merits closer attention.

Who then is this Herr Brauxel and what, really, are his *Erkenntnisbrillen*? The enigmatic Brauxel, alias Brauchsel, alias Brauksel, alias Hermann Haseloff, alias Goldmäulchen is, in addition to being a manufacturer, really an *artist*, we discover, by the name of Eduard Amsel. Amsel, a sculptor, primarily, but later a ballet director as well, is now also an author, the main fictive narrator of Grass' novel. And all of Amsel's artistic constructions (including Brauxel's eyeglasses which are in the same category) follow the same essential pattern: Though dealing exclusively with real life (just as the glasses show that which really happened in the nazi era) they strip away or peer beneath its facades and thereby capture the truly sordid essence hidden below. Consequently Amsel's artistic creations are often grotesque monstrosities, surpassing in shock effect all those devils and demons of the medieval allegorists, of Jan Brueghel or Albrecht Dürer, but all the more terrifying to man and beast precisely because they reveal real horrors, not imaginary ones. Amsel is, then, in a word, a mimetic mantic, an aesthetic seer like Klaff, a Beckmann-turned-artist who captures his terrible vision and passes it on to others with 'normal' vision, frozen into various *'objets d'art.'*

Amsel has possessed his mantic vision and attempted to 'freeze' it into art since early childhood, we discover. But due to their terrifying side effects—though hardly intended by him to become such—his very first sculptural creations were purchased, not by patrons of the arts, but by practical local farmers for use as scarecrows:

> Vogelscheuchen! Hier wird behauptet, der kleine Eduard Amsel habe anfangs—und als fünfeinhalbjähriger etwa baute er seine erste nennenswerte Scheuche—nicht die Absicht gehabt, Vogelscheuchen zu bauen . . . alle die ihm zuschauten . . . dachten aber in diese Richtung.[20]

Again, though he demonstrates great phantasy in their creation, it is their *realism*, that quintessential reality of the objects he copies, captured through Amsel's unique optical perspective, which gives his statues their powerful effect:

---

[20] *Ibid.*, p. 33.

> Wenn all diese vergänglichen Bauwerke immer wieder Fleiss und Anteil des Baumeisters verrieten, *war es dennoch Eduard Amsels wacher Sinn für die vielgestaltete Realität, war es sein über feisten Wangen neugieriges Auge,* das seine Produkte mit *gutbeobachteten* Details ausstattete, funktionieren liess und zu vogelscheuchenden Produkten machte. . . .[21]

When Amsel is about eight he uses willow branches to make a statue of his friend Walter Matern's sinister grandmother, which is then rented as a scarecrow by a certain farmer named Folchert. Folchert places it in his yard near the road, across from the Matern's vegetable garden, where it is seen by horses, cows and Lorchen Matern, feeble-minded victim of her sadistic grandmother's daily beatings with a large wooden spoon:

> Es zeigte sich bald, dass die Leihscheuche nicht nur Vögel vertrieb; Pferde liess sie scheuen und funkenschlagend durchgehen. Kühe, auf dem Weg zum Stall, versprengte es, sobald die löffelschwingende Weide ihren Schatten warf. Zu all dem verwirrten Vieh gesellte sich das arme Lorchen mit dem krausen Haar, das tagtäglich unter der echten löffelschwingenden Grossmutter zu leiden hatte. Nun wurde es von einer weiteren, dazu dreiköpfigen und weidenmässig aufgeputzten Grossmutter erschreckt und dergestalt in die Zange genommen, dass es windig und aufgelöst durch die Felder und den Strandwald, über die Dünen und Deiche, durch Haus und Garten irrte und einmal beinahe in das gehende Rutenzeug der Maternschen Bockwindmühle geraten wäre, hätte Lorchens Bruder, der Müller Matern, Lorchens Schürze nicht zu fassen bekommen. . . . Gegen den Willen des alten Folchert, der später prompt einen Teil der Leihgebühr zurückverlangte, mussten Walter Matern und Eduard Amsel die Scheuche über Nacht zerstören. *Es hatte also ein Künstler zum erstenmal begreifen müssen, dass seine Werke, wenn sie nur intensiv genug der Natur entnommen waren, nicht nur Macht über die Vögel unter dem Himmel hatten, sondern auch Pferden und Kühen, desgleichen dem armen Lorchen, also dem Menschen, die ländlich ruhige Gangart stören konnten.*[22]

Amsel's creations are terrifying because the realities—

---

[21] *Ibid.*
[22] *Ibid.*, p. 48.

the people, attitudes, deeds and situations—they represent are terrifying when reduced by Amsel's optics to their quintessential nature. Thus the young Amsel experiences a private (and subtle) vision of future pogroms and ritualistic burnings—synagogues, books, art objects, human beings?—when he is finally forced by his bigoted and superstitious neighbors to destroy all his scarecrows, including one especially terrible large bird made (perhaps significantly?) of tar and feathers: *der grosse Vogel Piepmatz*, as well as all of his collected raw materials: old clothes, sticks, wigs, hats and shoes. As his mound of junk goes up in flames and as the mob looking on taunts Amsel with increasingly anti-Semitic jibes, the *'Seher'* peers through *'Seh*schlitze' at this reality as though through an interior *Erkenntnisbrille* and sees that one day he will imitate in his art the apocalyptic realities of holocaust and doomsday:

> Von Kriwes Hand mit Kriwes Sturmfeuerzeug entzündet, greift das Feuer schnell um sich. Alle treten paar Schrittchen hinter sich, bleiben aber und wollen Zeuge der grossen Verbrennung sein. Während Walter Matern, wie immer bei Staatsaktionen [!] geräuschvoll tut und durch blosses Zähneknirschen das Prasseln zu übertönen versucht, steht Eduard Amsel, 'Posamentenmacher' genannt, und von Zeit zu Zeit, auch während der lustigen Verbrennung *'Itzich'* gerufen, lässig auf Sommersprossenbeinen, reibt eifrig die gepolsterten Handballen aneinander, *verkneift die Äugelchen und sieht etwas*. Kein grüngelber Qualm, kein schmorendes Lederzeug, kein glühender Funken- und Mottenflug zwingt ihn, *aus runden Augen quere Sehschlitze zu machen;* vielmehr beschenkt ihn der vielzüngig brennende Vogel, dessen Qualm niederschlägt und über Brennesseln kriecht, mit quicken Ideen. . . . Denn wie das entzündete Tier, Geburt aus Lumpen, Teer und Federn, sprühend, prasselnd und höchst lebendig einen letzten Flugversuch macht, dann stiebend in sich zusammenfällt, hat Amsel bei sich und in seinem Diarium beschlossen, später, wenn er mal gross ist, die Idee des Vogels Piepmatz wieder aufzunehmen: einen Riesenvogel will er bauen, der immerzu brennt, päsert und funkert, der dennoch nie verbrennt, sondern ewig, immer und von Natur, *apokalyptisch und dekorativ zugleich*, brennt, päsert und funkert.[23]

---

[23] *Ibid.*, p. 79f.

From this time forth until the advent of nazism, Eddi Amsel refrains from making any more sculptures 'from nature.' But when a group of young brown-shirts stage a mock battle for a pennant on the meadow behind his house and then return the next night to throw stones through his window, Eddi begins to sketch them and make small sculptural models of

> ringende Figurengruppen, ein Kuddelmuddel, ein formloses Geraufe, kurzbehost kniebestrumpft schulterberiemt braunbefetzt wimpelverrückt runenbenäht koppelverrutscht führergeimpft pimpfenmager heisergesiegt naturgetreu, wie unser Jungzug es in Amsels Garten beim Kampf um den Wimpel getrieben hatte. Amsel war es gelungen, den Zugang zur Realität wiederzufinden; fortan bastelte er keine modischen Schablonen mehr, Atelierpflanzen und Zimmerlinden, sondern ging auf die Strasse, neugierig und ausgehungert.[24]

Now Amsel "zeigte sich versessen auf Uniformen, besonders auf schwarze und braune, die mehr und mehr zum Strassenbild gehörten."[25] In order to obtain some old nazi uniforms Amsel asks his communist friend Matern to join the SA, which he eventually and reluctantly does (only to find to his delight many of his old Red Front buddies already there). Thanks to Amsel's ample checkbook, Matern is able to give twenty of his comrades new uniforms for old and he delivers the latter to Amsel's oak-paneled workroom. (Precisely because his art is based on reality, for Amsel the "Bierflecke, Fettflecke, Blutflecke, Teer- und Schweissflecke machten ihm die Koddern wertvoll.") Now, with his peculiar visionary optics the seer

> sortierte, zählte, stapelte, nahm Abstand, träumte von marschierenden Kolonnen, liess vorbeiziehen, grüssen vorbeiziehen, grüssen, *sah mit verkniffenen Augen*: Saalschlachten, Bewegung, Durcheinander, Menschen gegen Menschen, Knochen und Tischkanten, Augen und Daumen, Bierflaschen und Zähne, Schreie, stürzende Klaviere, Zierpflanzen, Kronleuchter und über zweihundertfünfzig

---

[24] *Ibid.*, p. 170.
[25] *Ibid.*, p. 171.

Onkel Walter und Papa auch, in den Schnee, und soviel Zähne werden gespuckt, eins zwei fünf dreizehn zweiunddreissig!²⁸

III

It would be instructive to pursue here one of the levels of symbolism Günter Grass had in mind when he adapted the postwar German *Gasmaskenbrille* and converted it into Brauxel's artistic *Erkenntnisbrille*. A clue to this particular symbolical—in fact almost allegorical—stratum is found in a passage of *Hundejahre* describing certain legal problems which arose after the eyeglasses began to be marketed. Investigative commissions in two German federal states took up the matter, we read, only to be dissolved when *"Gutachten berufener* Chemiker bestätigen *Wissenschaft*liches" about "das zu unrecht inkriminierte Modell":

> Die von den Ländern Niedersachsen und *Hessen* angestrengten *Verfahren* werden eingestellt.... Kein böser Winkelfabrikant will die westdeutsche Nachkriegs*jugend verderben*. Weder die zuständige *Bundesprüfstelle* noch *einstweilige Verfügungen* sind zu informieren oder vonnöten.... ²⁹

The word *Hessen* is perhaps the most easily recognizable among all these (italicized) verbal hints to the solution of this particular riddle:

On September 28, 1962, while Günter Grass was writing *Hundejahre*, his previous work *Katz und Maus* (1961) became the object of a motion filed by the office of the *Hessian* Minister for Labor, Public Welfare and Health, addressed to the 'Bundesprüfstelle für *Jugendgefährdende* Schriften' asking that *Katz und Maus* be placed on the list of prohibited books. Grass' publisher, Hermann Luchterhand & Co. was duly informed and in-

---

²⁸ *Ibid.*, p. 410.
²⁹ *Ibid.*, p. 404f.

vited to attend the hearing. Luchterhand's attorney Dr. Benseler began immediately to request '*Gutachten* berufener *Wissenschaftler*'[30] among whom were Germanists Walter Jens, Fritz Martini, Wilhelm Emrich, Joseph Vogt and Walter Höllerer; a psychiatrist Emil Ottinger; authors Hans Magnus Enzensberger and Kasimir Edschmid; as well as feullitonists Karl Korn of the *Frankfurter Allgemeine* and Joachim Kaiser of the *Süddeutsche Zeitung*. Exactly two months after the filing of the first motion, and after some but not all of these *Gutachten* had been received by Luchterhand, *Oberregierungsrat* Schilling of the *Bundesprüfstelle* wrote Luchterhand that "Der Hessische Minister für Arbeit, Volkswohlfahrt und Gesundheitswesen hat mit Schreiben von 28. November 1962 den Antrag zurückgezogen. Ich habe das *Verfahren eingestellt*."

The verbatim or near-verbatim references in the novel to the legal documents filed in this case—*Verfahren eingestellt*, *Bundesprüfstelle*, *Jugend verderben/jugendgefährdend*, *Gutachten*, *Wissenschaftliches/Wissenschaftler*, *Hessen*[31]—together with the chronological coincidence of this affair with the writing of *Hundejahre* strongly suggest (even allowing for repetitious legal phraseology) that Grass had his own previous works in mind when he created the idea of the *Erkenntnisbrille*. If this is true it would follow that the spectacles which Grass/Amsel provides for the youth are, at least on this level, none other than his own historical novels (though not necessarily limited

---

[30] See Gert Loschütz, ed., *Von Buch zu Buch: Günter Grass in der Kritik* (Neuwied: Luchterhand, 1968), pp. 27–69.

[31] *Ibid.*, p. 67. The other investigation mentioned, on the part of the State of Lower Saxony, cannot be explained as neatly. There *was* one more legal complaint filed against *Katz und Maus* at about this same time, on June 23, 1962, by the right-wing polemicist Kurt Ziesel. It was eventually thrown out by the *Staatsanwalt* which would seem to make it fit the fictive reference that both complaints were dropped. Later, long after the publication of *Hundejahre*, what began with this dispute flared into a lengthy legal battle between Grass and Ziesel described in: Heinz Ludwig Arnold and Franz Joseph Görtz, eds., *Grass: Dokumente zur politischen Wirkung* (Munich: Edition Text+Kritik, 1971).

to these), in and through which they clearly see the past deeds—particularly in war—of their parents. The specific idea of (literary) works of art *qua* revelatory spectacles may have been suggested to Grass by Hans Magnus Enzensberger, whose review of *Die Blechtrommel* (1959) was cited in part by Dr. Benseler of Luchterhand in his first reply to the *Bundesprüfstelle*: "Wie man von gewissen Stoffen behauptet, sie seien blutbildend," wrote Enzensberger, "in eben demselben Sinn kann man vom dem Roman *Die Blechtrommel* sagen, er sei weltbildend. *Er verändert die Sehweise des Lesers.*"[32]

Further evidence that the eyeglasses have become, on this level at least, a 'concretization' of the contagious point of view of *engagé* artists like Grass is found in yet another passage describing more legal complications as well as the overall geographical sales pattern of Brauxel's toy:

> Brillenvorkommnisse sind im gesamten Gebiet der Bundesrepublik zu verzeichnen; doch nur zu Zusammenballungen erschreckender Dichte kommt es nur in den Bundesländern Nordrhein-Westfalen, Hessen und Niedersachsen, während im Südosten, sowie im Land Bayern die Brillen gleichmässig gestreut in den Handel kommen. Einzig im Land Schleswig-Holstein gibt es, von Kiel und Lübeck abgesehen, ganze Bezirke, in denen keine Brillen nachgewiesen werden können, denn dort, in den Kreisen Eutin, Rendsburg und Neumünster, haben sich die Behörden nicht gescheut, die Brillen kartonweise und frisch vom Händler weg zu beschlagnahmen. Die 'einstweilige Verfügung' wurde nachgeliefert. Zwar gelingt es der Firma Brauxel & Co., Schadenersatzansprüche geltend zu machen; aber nur in den Städten und in der Umgebung von Itzehoe vermögen die Brillen Kundschaft zu finden, die sich ein Bild macht, ein Elternbild.[33]

Shipments of *Katz und Maus*, *Die Blechtrommel* or any other artistic writings of the period were, to my knowledge, never

---

[32] *Ibid.*, p. 54.
[33] *Hundejahre*, p. 406f.

impounded, a reminder that Grass is not writing autobiographical allegory here, despite the close allusions in these passages to actual events and situations involving him. But, in fact, the atmosphere in the Federal Republic at the time of the writing of *Hundejahre* in the fall of 1962 *was* dominated by similar impoundings against other writers and formers of public opinion in the famous *Spiegel* affair.

On October 26, it will be recalled, the editors and publisher of that weekly newsmagazine were charged with treason and arrested and its offices were occupied by police. Before the smoke cleared, the conservative CDU administration of Konrad Adenauer had been terminally shaken and the Bavarian Franz Josef Strauss, the Federal Minister of Defense, had grudgingly admitted complicity in the matter and immediately resigned. One of the key terms which occurs twice in the passages by Grass cited above: "einstweilige Verfügung" (a temporary restraining injunction) fairly begs, in this context, to be read as a reference to Strauss and to his penchant for suspending normal civil liberties like freedom of speech and of the press by arranging for such injunctions. Even when the rather more conservative paper *Die Welt* wished to caricature Strauss at about this time they chose to portray him festooned with placards bearing the term "einstweilige Verfügung" above the ironic caption: "Kein Prozesshansl."[34]

The act of seizing Brauxel's eyeglasses then, would seem to stand for all the acts of those public servants like Strauss who would intervene in the process of enlightenment, as Grass views it, who would act to prevent "die Sehweise" of Germans, particularly young Germans, from being changed in the way the toy glasses are purported to do and in the manner Grass, *Der Spiegel, et al.* were attempting.

---

[34] As reprinted in *Der Spiegel*, March 28, 1962, p. 16.

Other indications that the spectacles represent all these kinds of efforts to influence the point of view of young people (including their political views) are found in a book edited at about this same time (1961) by Martin Walser: *Die Alternative oder Brauchen wir eine neue Regierung?* to which Grass contributed a short essay entitled: "Wer wird dieses Bändchen kaufen?" Here the metaphor is auditory, not visual, but there are other parallels to the eyeglasses. The Bavarian bogy-man Strauss is again invoked, as are a class of young book purchasers in the same age-group as those who purchase Brauxel's *Erkennungsbrille:* "Wieviele Neuwähler gibt es? Denen will ich ins Ohr kriechen und in jeder Milchbar flüstern: Wählt SPD und möbelt die alte Tante auf, sonst kommt jener Vormund aus Bayern." "Weiterhin," Grass continues (with yet another, albeit more ironic reference linking his books to the glasses),

> —und die Höhe meiner Auflagezahlen verpflichtet mich dazu— spreche ich zu allen, die die 'Blechtrommel' gelesen oder zumindest gekauft haben. Nicht, dass ich sagen will, Oskar Matzerath wählt SPD, aber sein Sohn und Halbbruder Kurt—Sie erinnern sich?— ein blasses, inzwischen wahlberechtigtes Bengelchen, hat mir versprochen, wieder fleissig zur Kirche zu gehen und SPD zu wählen; ein Beweis mehr, wie einflussreich Schriftsteller sein können.[35]

If Grass is indeed attempting with the magic spectacles to promote along with his own particular point of view that of the Social Democratic Party, then it should not surprise us that the geographical areas mentioned above in connection with the sales of the glasses seem to correspond exactly to the success and failure of the SPD in the years immediately preceeding 1963, the publication date of *Hundejahre*. In Nordrhein-Westfalen, for example, listed in *Hundejahre* as a place

---

[35] Martin Walser, *Die Alternative oder Brauchen wir eine neue Regierung?* (Hamburg: rororo, 1961). Also quoted in Arnold and Görtz, *Grass: Dokumente zur politischen Wirkung,* p. 3f.

where the glasses sold well, the SPD—after polling as low as 31.4% in 1949 and 33.5% in 1957—received 37.3% in the federal elections of 1961 and 43.3% in the state elections held in 1962. It made even more progress in Hesse and in Lower Saxony.³⁶ In places where fewer glasses were sold, however, —"während im Südosten sowie im Land Bayern die Brillen gleichmässig gestreut in den Handel kommen"—just the opposite is found. But even in Bavaria there are still *some* glasses sold, we read, whereas "Einzig im Land Schleswig-Holstein gibt es, von Kiel und Lübeck abgesehen, ganze Bezirke, in denen keine Brillen nachgewiesen werden können . . ."³⁷ If our interpretation of the correlation between the eyeglasses and the antifascist point of view is correct, then this must be an oblique reference to Schleswig-Holstein's popular reputation as a haven for nazi war criminals and neonazi movements as depicted in a typical cartoon of the era, reprinted from the *Stuttgarter Zeitung* in a *Spiegel* article of May 10, 1961 (pp. 24-33) entitled: "Schleswig-Holstein und seine Nazis." Here, a government official surrounded by the Schleswig-Holstein coat of arms slyly winks at Adolf Hitler and says: "So, Schickelgruber heissen Sie? —Ja, dann steht Ihrer Bewerbung bei uns nichts im Wege."

IV

But there exists yet another symbolical dimension to Grass' eyeglasses, on a level different from the sales pattern of *engagé* books or the demographic fortunes of the SPD, a first reference to which occurs in the description of Brauxel's manufacturing process:

---

[36] For all the pertinent election data see Egon Klepsch *et al.*, eds., "Wahlergebnisse seit 1946," *Die Bundestagswahl 1965, Geschichte und Staat*, volume 109 (Munich: Olzog, 1965), pp. 146–160.
[37] *Hundejahre*, p. 407.

> Nur die Gläser müssen, obgleich sie wie Fensterglas keinen besonderen Schliff aufweisen, das Ergebnis langer Forschungsarbeit sein. . . . Aber Brauxel & Co.—ein übrigens angesehenes Unternehmen—kann beiden Untersuchungsausschüssen nachweisen, dass kein Optiker laborierte, dass allenfalls die kleine, dem Werk angeschlossene Glashütte eine besondere und deshalb als Patent gemeldete Mischung zum Schmelzen bringt: dem wohlbekannten Gemenge Quarzsand, Soda, Glaubersalz und Kalkstein wird eine aufs Gramm gewogene und deshalb geheimzuhaltende Dosis Glimmer, wie er von Glimmergneisen, Glimmerschiefer und Glimmergranit gewonnen wird, beigemengt . . . und dennoch muss irgend etwas dran sein an den Dingern—*die beigemengten Glimmerspiegelchen werden's wohl sein*—aber nur die Jugend, die Siebenjährigen bis Einundzwanzigjährigen kapieren den Trick, denn ein Trick wohnt in den Brillen, den weder Erwachsene noch Kleinkinder zu begreifen vermögen.[38]

One of the most important interpretive clues here to the symbolism of Brauxel's 'trick' is the term *Glimmerspiegelchen* which, petrologically speaking, refers to those minute, flaky crystals of mica found in quartz, feldspar and hornblende (as well as in gneis, slate and granite, hence: "Glimmergneis, Glimmerschiefer, Glimmergranit").

These particular *Glimmerspiegelchen*, key ingredient in Brauxel's formula for the lenses, have been extracted, we confidently infer, from stones collected over his entire lifetime by an eccentric teacher named Oswald Brunies (for after Brunies' death in the concentration camp 'Haseloff' returns from Berlin, loads a large truck with his stones and sends them to the potash mine, the site of his future factory). Brunies has always been one of the teachers to accompany Amsel and Walter on their annual class outing to the school's boarding lodge in the Saskoschin Forest near the Polish border where lives a secluded band of gypsies, with whom only Brunies has secret contacts, and with whom he regularly barters for wild honey (to make the malt candy to which he is addicted), as well

---

[38] *Ibid.*, p. 405.

as for micaseous rocks. Hence, by a process of rather subtle concatenation, the mica *Spiegelchen* from Brunies' special stones and the eyeglasses made with them seem to have something of the mystery and lore of the gypsy about them, and we begin to wonder if Grass intends his readers to associate the romantic Brunies' stones, their magical *Glimmerspiegelchen* and Brauxel's spectacles with gypsy crystal balls.

Our suspicions are deepened when we discover that Brauxel also consumes these *Spiegelchen* in his hot lemonade—doubtless contributing to or renewing the power of his *interior Erkenntnisbrille*—brewed for him like a magic potion by Jenny Angustri, a foundling child given to Brunies by the Saskoschin gypsies, who also adds other secret ingredients, all according to a 'gypsy recipe':

> Denn was dieses Gläschen voller Üblichem zu Besonderem macht, sind nicht auserwählte Zitronen und Extrawasser: eine Messerspitze Glimmer, von Glimmergneisen und Glimmergranit gewonnen, wird dem Glas—achten Sie bitte auf die silbrigen Fischchen!—beigemengt, alsdann—ich verrate Ihnen ein *Zigeunerrezept*—stimmen drei Tropfen kostbar köstliche Essenz, die meine liebe Jenny jederzeit für mich übrig hat, dieses mein Lieblingsgetränk *zauberisch*, dass es wie Balsam durch meine Kehle rinnt.[39]

Even the term *Spiegelchen* itself (a reference as well to *Der Spiegel*?) seems to have been carefully chosen as we perceive upon turning to Theodore Besterman's standard work on *Crystal-Gazing*. From Besterman we learn that crystallomancy is "not originally one of the common forms of scrying, though now practically the only one used (the usual name of scrying, crystal-gazing, speaking for itself)," but that catoptromancy or enoptromancy, on the other hand, "has probably been the most widely used of all methods of scrying."[40] Gypsy crystal-

---

[39] *Ibid.*, p. 471.
[40] Theodore Besterman, *Crystal-Gazing. A Study in the History, Distribution, Theory and Practice of Scrying* (New Hyde Park: University Books, 1965), p. 2f.

lomancy, it would appear, is merely a variant of *mirror scrying* or catoptromancy, itself related to and perhaps derived from lithomancy or the use of shew stones, peep stones or seer stones, all of which together seem to be suggested by Brunies' gypsy stones and the *Spiegelchen* extracted from them which form the key ingredient in the lenses of the *Wunderbrille* produced by the seer Brauxel.

Even the term *Brille* itself, like its English equivalent 'spectacles' it would now appear, fits neatly into this symmetrical symbolical construct: both terms have their origin in the realm of catoptromancy and lithomancy. Just as the English word 'spectacles' is related to Latin *speculum* 'mirror' (cf. German *Spiegel*), the German term *Brille* directly derives from Greek βήρυλλος (*béryllos*), a sea-green gem (of which emerald and aquamarine are two varieties) used originally by "Brillenseher"[41] or 'beryl-seers' for miraculously viewing otherwise invisible things, i.e., for scrying.[42]

---

[41] See the *Oxford English Dictionary* under 'spectacle,' and the Grimms' *Deutsches Wörterbuch* under 'brille' (especially as "wahrsagerglas"), as well as under 'brillenseher.' Also see Webster's *New World Dictionary* (College Edition only) which lists 'Beryl' as a feminine name meaning "prophetic soothsayer."

[42] Interestingly, the history of eyeglasses itself has been difficult to write because modern spectacles—valued only for their non-magical optical properties—emerged gradually (in a somewhat analogous manner perhaps to modern chemistry emerging from alchemy or astronomy from astrology) from magical scrying beryls, whose users eventually made the empirical discovery that such stones were empowered not only to bring future, past, distant or otherwise hidden events into focus, but, when placed near small writing or other diminutive detail-work such as that on tapestries or jewelry, made these more visible as well. Naturally any such discoveries were kept as quiet as possible, something about which Edward Jackson doubtless quite correctly conjectures: "When Alexander de Spina of Pisa [the first person known to describe—in 1313—a pair of eyeglasses] was said to have seen a pair of spectacles worn by someone who made a secret of their invention, such secrecy might well have been based on a desire to avoid the dangers of charges of witchcraft" ("Historical Evolution and Use of Spectacles," *American Journal of Opthalmology*, 1927, Series 3, number 10, pp. 605–608). See also a lengthy monograph with many references to other works on the subject by Edward Rosen, "The Invention of Eyeglasses," *Journal of the History of Medicine*, January 1956, pp. 13–46 and April 1956, pp. 183–218.

Without being able to recount here the entire *corpus* of lore surrounding scrying, crystal balls, seer stones, magic mirrors, the phenomenon called 'second sight' and many other related folkloric and literary occurrences ranging from "Spieglein, Spieglein an der Wand. . ." to Faust's vision in a magic mirror in the witch's kitchen,[43] it suffices for our purposes to suspect rather strongly that Günter Grass intends to evoke some or all this lore in association with his *Erkenntnisbrille*, thus adding at least two other dimensions to the relatively straightforward motif of the *Gasmaskenbrille* as he inherited it. The first dimension is the simplest and has been touched on before: Now Grass' works (and the *engagé* works of other postwar writers as well, including, perhaps, even *Der Spiegel*), appear as mirrors held up to the Third Reich and to postwar German society. Each individual *Glimmerspiegelchen* in the *Erkenntnisbrille*/literary work illuminates one hidden facet of reality, that is, it imparts one 'glimmer' of insight to the wearer/reader.

But what about the other dimension? Why must these mirrors be *magical* mirrors? Perhaps there is no good reason for them to be magical except that Grass liked it that way, or perhaps there are good reasons of which I am not aware. My best answer to that question is that like their paradoxical an-

---

A chap-book written as late as 1627 accused Roger Bacon (1214?–1294), one of the fathers of modern optics, with possession of "A brazen head and a magical glass," by means of which—in terms strikingly premonitory of Brauxel's *Wunderbrille*—"Fathers did oftentimes desire to see how their Children did, and Children how their Parents did." Cited by Besterman, *Crystal-Gazing*, p. 14.

[43] Besterman's *Crystal-Gazing*; a book by Lewis Spence on *Second-Sight* (London: Rider & Co., 1951); a monograph on magical stones, especially in German Romanticism ("Der Karfunkelstein," *Euphorion* 55, 1961, pp. 297–326) and a book about magical mirrors (*Disenchanted Images, A Literary Iconology*, Princeton: Princeton University Press, 1977), both by Theodore Ziolkowski; along with such standard reference works as Stith Thompson's *Motif-Index of Folk Literature* or Hanns Bächtold-Stäubli's *Handwörterbuch des deutschen Aberglaubens* provide a good introduction to this vast subject.

cestors the seer stones and scrying mirrors, these *Wunderbrillen*, whose very *raison d'être* is to enlighten, have their origins (and are very much at home) in the dark world of magic and superstition. So it is precisely this, their paradoxical, antipodal character that would make them a fitting symbol for postwar German writers. Wishing to enlighten the present world about the hidden deeds of the nazi past, yet desiring to deal with the past on its own occult and irrational terms, for the postwar German artist like Grass the magical revelatory eyeglasses (and all that they represent) could be the perfect 'bifocal' mediator between the two worlds.

Stating the matter in a slightly different way, one could say that whereas conventional histories of the Third Reich and its aftermath may attempt to enlighten by viewing their subject rationally and empirically, often enough in outright positivistic terms of social, economic and political cause-and-effect, the *artistic* histories of the Third Reich with which we are dealing here—while also wishing to enlighten—choose to do so by allowing the wearer of the magical spectacles to look directly in on and experience this bizarre world literally (to borrow from von Ranke) "wie es eigentlich gewesen." And since it is a Faustian world which "hat sich der Magie ergeben,"[44] this is, ultimately, the reason why the *Gasmaskenbrille* must become a *Wunderbrille*: only as such can it be totally at home in a cosmos given over to magic, myth, superstition and religiosity run amok, as Joachim Fest recounts:

> Die Neigung, ausserhalb der Realität nach Zeichen und Hoffnungen zu suchen, griff mit dem näherrückenden Ende. . . um sich und offenbarte noch einmal die modernitätsverdeckte Irrationalität des Nationalsozialismus. Ley machte sich in den ersten Apriltagen erregt zum Fürsprecher eines Erfinders von 'Todesstrahlen,' Goebbels holte sich Auskunft in zwei Horoskopen, und

---

[44] *Hundejahre*, p. 54. This is also, of course, Thomas Mann's central metaphor in *Dr. Faustus* for Germany's nazi experience.

während die amerikanischen Truppen schon das Alpenvorland erreichten, Schleswig-Holstein abgeschnitten wurde und Wien verlorenging, flackerten aus Planetenkonjunktionen, Aszendenzen und Transiten im Quadrat noch einmal Hoffnung auf eine grosse Wende in der zweiten Aprilhälfte empor. Noch ganz erfüllt von diesen Parallelen und Prognosen erfuhr Goebbels am 13. April . . . dass der amerikanische Präsident Roosevelt gestorben sei. 'Er war in Ekstase,' hat einer der Miterlebenden geschildert und liess sich augenblicklich mit dem Führerbunker verbinden: 'Mein Führer, ich gratuliere Ihnen,' rief er in den Apparat. 'Es steht in den Sternen geschrieben, dass die zweite Aprilhälfte für uns den Wendepunkt bringen wird!'[45]

In any clear mirroring of such a cosmos, where there also existed a carefully orchestrated mystical cult of the *Führer*, the messiah, the savior of Germany,[46] is it any wonder that a moral gnome like Oskar Matzerath has his own messiah complex? That Brauxel's eyeglasses are *magical* or that he is a numerologist?[47] Is it any wonder that Brauxel consults the stars and bases some of his most apocalyptic constructs on astrological patterns like that of the 'Great Conjunction in the Sign of Aquarius?' This, then, is perhaps the ultimate exegetical value of our discussion about the eyeglasses of postwar German literature: Just as those characters around Beckmann insisted—and quite correctly at that—that his spectacles were hideous, all the while ignoring the more hideous reality of which they were a mere reflection; so too, on occasion, have the magical eyeglasses (read: *engagé* works of art) of postwar Germany been mistaken for that reality they attempt to portray.

---

[45] Joachim Fest, *Hitler: Eine Biographie* (Frankfurt: Propyläen, 1973), p. 1000 ff.

[46] *Ibid.*, pp. 354, 287.

[47] Hitler engaged in numerological schemes like picking the magical 7 as his membership number in the German Workers Party even though he was the 55th person to join. (Actually, since the system began with 501, he bore membership number 555.) See Joachim Fest, *Hitler*, p. 227 and Werner Maser, *Adolf Hitler* (Munich: Bechtle, 1971), p. 462, note 225: "Hitler's Behauptung, die Mitgliedsnummer 7 bekommen zu haben, hat später einen erheblichen Beitrag zur Bildung des Hitler-Kultes geliefert."

So when Günter Grass' works, for example, alternately motivate legal proceedings alleging pornography or blasphemy[48] and lengthy numerological and mythological scholarly hairsplitting,[49] we suspect again that the medium is being mistaken for the message, the seismograph for the earthquake and the (dark) glass for its (clear) image of an even darker era.

---

[48] As in the case of Kurt Ziesel or the state of Hesse.
[49] Like Michael Harscheidt's 758-page *Günter Grass, Wort-Zahl-Gott* (Bonn: Bouvier, 1976) or Edward Diller's *A Mythic Journey, Günter Grass' Tin Drum* (Lexington: University of Kentucky Press, 1974).

CHAPTER TWO

The Symbolical Limp and the Secular Postwar Seer

I

The reader may have already noticed that another attribute held in common by almost all those wearers of interior or exterior *Erkenntnisbrillen* is their limp. Borchert's Beckmann, Walser's Berthold Klaff, Böll's Alfred Schrella and Lenz' Man in the Hotel[1] all share this same infirmity, and these four protagonists are only the tip of a veritable iceberg of literary limpers. Indeed, it may not be going too far to say that postwar German literature is virtually crawling with hobbling heroes. Friedrich Dürrenmatt's 'Old Lady,' several of Böll's clowns like Hans Schnier and Wilhelm Bechthold, as well as Grass' hunchback Oskar Matzerath and his teethgnasher Walter Matern come to mind immediately.[2] Many others could be listed, for in this case—unlike that of the eyeglasses—we have

---
[1] See chapter one.
[2] Friedrich Dürrenmatt, *Der Besuch der alten Dame* (Zürich: Arche, 1956); Heinrich Böll, *Ansichten eines Clowns* (Cologne: Kiepenheuer & Witsch, 1963); Heinrich Böll, *Entfernung von der Truppe* (Cologne: Kiepenheuer & Witsch, 1964), especially p. 31: "Besondere Merkmale: leichter Schräggang (wegen des Schusses in die Hüfte."); Günter Grass, *Die Blechtrommel* (Neuwied: Luchterhand, 1959).

the good fortune of being able to draw on an almost exhaustive compendium of limpers in world literature.[3] Granted, his specialty being American literature, Peter Hays has overlooked a few postwar German hobblers, but his book is nonetheless helpful for locating our motif in earlier German as well as in world literature generally.

One of the problems arising for Hays out of such a superabundance of literary limpers, of course (he lists several hundred, from Ahab to Oedipus, Mephistopheles to *Gunsmoke's* Chester Good, Achilles to Tiny Tim, and Toller's Hinkemann to Kleist's Judge Adam), is that he finds it difficult to categorize them all meaningfully and to determine to what degree, if any, each fictional character assumes, by virtue of his membership in 'the ancient guild of limpers' any deeper, symbolical dimensions. In the last analysis, the infirmities of a vast majority of the lame and the halt identified by Mr. Hays seem to him very simply to represent incompleteness, inadequacy, impotency, castration, or sometimes evil. But there is a smaller, more enigmatic group of limpers upon which he bases the first (and most interesting) part of his book: the group composed of those who rise above the level of impotent cripple to earn renewed virility, fulfillment, wisdom and favor with God, and who retain the limp as a sacred relic.

An early example of this kind of emblematic limp is described in the Old Testament, in Genesis 32, where Jacob wrestles with a divine being. After a night-long struggle, his anonymous assailant finally succeeds in putting his leg out of joint by "touching the hollow" of Jacob's thigh. But when Jacob continues to refuse to let him go, "except thou bless me," his opponent then reveals his divine identity and says that Jacob should henceforth be called Israel (from *sarah* 'to fight'

---

[3] Peter L. Hays, *The Limping Hero* (New York: New York University Press, 1971).

and *el* 'God'[4]), "denn du hast mit Gott und mit Menschen gekämpft und bist obgelegen." And although the King James Version here tends to obscure the identity of Jacob's opponent by its rendering "for as a prince hast thou power with God and with men" (hence the above quotation from the Luther Bible), it does have Jacob say "I have seen God face to face, and my life is preserved" before he "halted upon his thigh" away from that place which he calls Peniel ('face of God') "as the sun rose upon him." Though he is injured in his battle, Jacob ascends from it to a new, more meaningful existence, here symbolized by the rising sun; endowed by virtue of his nocturnal struggles with deeper understanding of life. He limps not out of any inadequacy or inherent evil, then, but as a symbol of his enhanced prosperity and fertility.[5]

Peter Hays continues his analysis by citing Robert Graves who, in his semifictional mythology, diagnoses Jacob's injury as "an inward displacement of the hip, first described by Hippocrates, and once common to wrestlers."[6] Graves quotes Arab lexicographers to demonstrate that a person so injured could walk only on his toes, in a lurching or swaggering gait, unable to touch his heel to the ground. Then,

---

[4] Cf. *The New Bible Dictionary* under 'Israel.' (Grand Rapids: Eerdmans, 1962).

[5] The English translation undoubtedly gives rise to the popular idea that Jacob wrestled with an angel. But see also Hosea 12:4.

Jacob's divine laming, involved as it was with that symbolic Old Testament organ of procreation, the thigh (Hebrew *yarekh*, usually translated 'loins', cf. Hays pp. 11–15), seems to be prefigured in a rite revealed to his grandfather Abram (Genesis 17), where God's covenant with Abram, including the promise to "multiply him exceedingly" is sealed by the initiation of the ritual of circumcision. After receiving this promise of renewed procreative power, 99-year-old Abram's name was changed to Abraham, 'father of many nations,' just as that of his grandson was to be later changed to Israel when God touched "the hollow of his *yarekh*" to ensure the propogation of his, and hence Abraham's, seed.

[6] Robert Graves, "The Bull-Footed God," *The White Goddess* (London: Faber and Faber, 1948) especially pp. 313–340.

using Hosea 12:3 as evidence, Graves shows that the incident which occurred at the birth of Jacob and his twin Esau—"Jacob's hand took hold on Esau's heel"[7]—is connected with his subsequent laming and with the name Jacob, which is, according to Graves, *Jah-aceb*, 'the Heel God.' This 'tripping up of Esau's heel' (as the Septuagint has it) clearly foreshadows the purchase of Esau's birthright, the fight with God and *Jah-aceb's* laming. For Graves, then, Jacob fits perfectly the pattern of the legendary Sacred King who always succeeds to office by tripping up a rival: "Sacred Kings, it seems, were not allowed to rest their heels on the ground, but walked on their toes like the Canaanite Agag."[8] But it is not only the laming which causes Jacob to fit the pattern of a Sacred King; the King's laming always signified the renewal of his fertility, an attribute then passed on by him to the crops, flocks and homes of his realm.

These myths of the Sacred King can be traced ultimately, Graves postulates, to the legend of the marriage between the Sun King and the Earth Queen, which depicts his death as a member of his former tribe and his rebirth with a new name into that of his Queen. "Originally," he says, "the King died violently as soon as he had coupled with the Queen; as the drone dies after coupling with the queen bee. Later, emasculation and laming were substituted for death; later still, circumcision was substituted for emasculation and the wearing of

---

[7] Genesis 25:26.

[8] The κόθορνος (*cóthornos*) or high-heeled buskin of another Sacred King, Dionysos, later worn by actors in the Greek theatre in honor of him, can also be explained when one considers with Graves that his name probably meant 'the lame God of light', or that another of his titles, μηροτράφής (*Merotrāphés*) means very simply 'one whose thigh is taken very good care of,' from μηρός (*merós*) 'thigh' and τρέφω (*trépho*) 'to tend or nurse, to take care of.' Likewise, Hermes' winged sandals, like those of Theseus and Perseus, "were probably not so much a symbol of swiftness but a sign of the holiness of the heel, and so, paradoxically, a symbol of lameness." *The White Goddess*, pp. 329, 323.

buskins for laming."⁹ Various remnants of these ancient practices, Graves maintains, account for other, more familiar lamings, especially in the Bible, where earlier legends became iconotropically reinterpreted after the Hebrews captured at Hebron a set of icons depicting the ritual fate of the Sacred King. And so, through this somewhat roundabout way, Graves arrives at what is perhaps the most interesting of all lamings.

In his book *King Jesus*[10] he describes Christ's crucifixion as a Roman ritual borrowed from the Canaanite Carthaginians, which was in fact a remnant of the annual ritualistic killing of the Sacred King. In this particular rite, the nail was driven in to pin the foot of the victim to the side of the cross—not the front—and was probably placed between the Achilles (!) tendon and the ankle bone. After Christ's resurrection (Sacred Kings had not actually been killed for centuries, Graves reminds us) he must have limped on his toes, Graves deduces, to avoid placing his heels with their sacred wounds on the ground. Graves presses the idea of a limping Jesus still further, postulating a secret coronation ceremony on Mount Tabor during which Jesus was lamed in a ritualistic wrestling match; citing St. Jerome's statement that Jesus was deformed; and referring to the tradition of the *Talmud Babli Sanhedrin* and the *Tol' Doth Yeshu* that Jesus was lamed while attempting to flee. But Graves is not the only author to treat the resurrected Jesus as a limper.[11]

---

[9] *The White Goddess*, p. 331. Sigmund Freud also shared this view, mentioning it in at least a dozen places. In *Der Mann Moses und die monotheistische Religion* he says: "Die Beschneidung ist der symbolische Ersatz der Kastration, die der Urvater einst aus der Fülle seiner Machtvollkommenheit über die Söhne verhängt hatte. . . . " *Gesammelte Werke* XVI (London: Imago, 1950), p. 230.

[10] Robert Graves, *King Jesus* (New York: Creative Age Press, 1946).

[11] Perhaps Graves pushes the idea too far, perhaps not. In one way I am tempted to go even further. When I read the account of Adam and Eve, especially Genesis 3:15, in connection with Graves' *(continued on page 40)*

In his short novel *The Man Who Died* (1928), D. H. Lawrence portrays Jesus awakening in the tomb before limping with "unspeakable pain" on hurt feet to the nearby home of a peasant. Then, like Adam, Abraham, Dionysos and Jacob, the limping God becomes fruitful: as the resurrected Osiris, in a new identity, he fructifies the womb of the priestess of Isis.

II

The mythic pattern thus roughly sketched out can, it seems, be reduced to the following paradigm: A normal individual is forced to engage in some form of combat where he suffers a laming wound. But rather than being incapacitated, he arises from the incident with a new identity, often mythic or universal; a new name, usually noble or divine; new insights; and, appropriately, newly increased powers of procreation. Ironically, those few English and American literary examples which Peter Hays believes come closest to fitting the paradigm by, in his words, "denoting fertility"[12] actually do not fit the paradigm—taken as a group—nearly as well as the postwar Germans, some examples of which we have already seen. All the postwar German protagonists like Beckmann, for example, have engaged in combat; most have new identities and new names, either in the negative sense ("Ich will nicht mehr

---

(continued from page 39) legends of the heel, it appears that the fall of Adam, often held to have been caused by the same coupling-act ascribed to the Sun King, rendered him and his posterity vulnerable to the laming bite of the serpent, who was given power to "bruise his heel," i.e. lame him. This laming, however, and later the related rite of circumcision were offset by Adam's new powers of procreation, definitely a 'blessing' in the sense that Abraham and Israel were blessed.

[12] In addition to Lawrence's *Man Who Died*, he lists Tennessee Williams' Brick Pollitt from *Cat on a Hot Tin Roof*; Adam Rosenzweig from Robert Penn Warren's *Wilderness*; Truman Capote's Mary O'Meaghan from "Among the Paths to Eden"; Sy Levin in Malamud's *A New Life* and Frank Alpine in his *The Assistant*; Dr. Pep in "Dr. Pep's Sermon" and Eugene Henderson in *Henderson the Rain King* by Saul Bellow.

Beckmann sein!") or in the positive (Brauxel/Haseloff/Goldmäulchen); and that all have emerged from their existential struggles with new insights is the very point of the exterior or interior *Erkenntnisbrillen*. Like the ancient prophets of the paradigm, too, these modern-day Jacobs are, as we have determined, mimetic mantics or secular seers, basing their 'soothsayings' on the linguistic, aesthetic and historical insights gained from their struggles with nazism.

In fact, only one characteristic of the paradigmatic limper does not immediately and obviously apply to the postwar German protagonists we have encountered: It is difficult at first glance to understand how a limping hero of the suicidal type like Klaff or Beckmann could have 'newly increased powers of procreation' since, far from being able or willing to create new life, they act to end even their own. This view, of course, is too narrow, too literal. Klaff and Beckmann, it will be recalled, though without literal heirs, have many symbolic ones, just as Böll's limper Alfred Schrella forms a new family with some of the Fähmels and other 'lambs' which are his kindred in spirit though not by blood. To clarify this point, however, it would be well to examine yet another hobbling hero, one who may be *the* archetypal postwar German limping seer par excellence: Anton Schmitz.

Schmitz, the protagonist of Paul Schallück's novel *Don Quichotte in Köln* (1967) is, like his famous Iberian namesake, an 'undoer of wrongs and injuries.' Unlike the famous knight of the rueful figure, however, it is not the ideals of chivalry that motivate him, but the ideals of humanity which he has proclaimed over the air for seven years in his capacity as editor of the program "Mensch und Menschlichkeit" at West German Radio and Television (WDR) in Cologne. One morning, about three weeks preceeding carnival, he inexplicably gets up before the alarm clock awakens him and lights a cigarette before eating breakfast, acts seriously upsetting to his traditional morning routine and to his aging mother, with whom he lives. Thereafter he stays in his room, pacing and mumbling, unshaven and sustained only by an occasional apple. Finally, on the Monday before Lent, he appears to give up his vigil and rest until noon on Shrove Tuesday when he prepares to go to the ball. At Cologne's famous Gürzenich ballroom he methodically looks upstairs and down until he finds a girl whom he addresses as *Claudia*. They embrace and kiss; but as he begins to speak to her "von der Würde, die die Lust versüsse, vom Glück der freien Wahl und von der Noblesse der Wahrhaftigkeit"[13] she begins to detach her body from his, and she disappears into the crowd. The rest of the night is spent searching for this or perhaps another 'Claudia.'

The next morning, Ash Wednesday, finds Anton perched on a traffic island in the middle of a street near the train station, a tin toy trumpet with a scrap of carnival poster for a mouthpiece in his hand. When he hears cries coming from behind some parked cars across the busy street, Schmitz concludes that an innocent girl is being violated. He calls through his homemade megaphone for the evildoer to cease his crime immediately. For his trouble Schmitz is abused physically by the man and verbally by the girl. Luckily a policeman is near, and Schmitz is rescued from the angry pair. For the "Kölner Don Quichotte" this is the first of many similar tilts with windmills—each time Schmitz attempts to aid or comfort another human being, but he is invariably rewarded with derision, hatred and often enough, contusions.

Slightly discouraged, Schmitz decides to ask his friend Peter Scheel, a sound-technician at the broadcast house to go with him on his future ventures. After much coaxing, Peter agrees to do so, and he and Schmitz set up headquarters in

---

[13] Paul Schallück, *Don Quichotte in Köln* (Frankfurt: Fischer, 1967), p. 10.

Scheel's bachelor apartment. Before dropping off to sleep for three days, the weary Schmitz instructs Scheel to bring his old bicycle from his apartment and to buy another to go with it. "Den alten Drahtesel?' Peter asks. "Den alten Drahtesel, kaufst noch einen dazu hier ist Geld," Anton replies. When the pair leaves the apartment four days later, it is fitting that this latter-day Sancho Panza is chosen to ride the old 'wire donkey' whereas Don Quixote mounts his more recent acquisition.

After two more adventures the pair disappears into a tavern. Since they are the only customers, the aging waiter takes the liberty of reading them a 'parable' which he has discovered in an illustrated weekly. Anton listens intently while Peter proceeds to slake his thirst. The title of the parable, written by someone named Paul Schallück, the waiter says, is "Von einem Manne, der das Gehen verlernt hat." The contents of this lengthy parable affect Anton so greatly that he immediately integrates it into his plan of action, basing the next phase of his endeavors almost entirely on his apparent interpretation of the allegory. The 'Man Who Has Forgotten How To Walk' is a driver who becomes a madman when he slides behind a steering wheel. He drove, the old waiter reads, "den stärksten Wagen seiner Zeit," and although he had previously lost his driver's license for over a decade "eines nie geklärten Unfalls wegen," he shows total disregard for the laws of traffic. One foggy day when he and two passengers are driving along the highway overtaking other vehicles with impunity, he attempts to pass four large trucks. In the ensuing collision one of the truck drivers and both of the man's passengers are killed, but he is found alive under one of the trucks. At the hospital he is patched together as well as possible, given transfusions and placed in immobilizing plaster casts. Although the hospital staff attempt to teach him the error of his ways by showing him photographs of traffic victims and orphans, he is unable to react to these "unerkennbare

Bündel auf den Fotos" and insists "das Manöver sei ihm aufgezwungen worden, bestimmt." But despite his inability to react to this spiritual therapy, his physical reserves are astounding. He heals so rapidly that people begin to speak in terms of a "Wunder." After a certain time the man is allowed to leave the hospital, and with the aid of crutches he is able to walk, dance, run, and march.

His firm had been forced to reduce its size, but his old father had stepped in and kept it above water and now he insists on retaining control. The man is allowed to roll about the offices in his wheelchair and make minor decisions, but his sons think it a shame that he should not be able to walk on his own, especially since his inability to do so has been determined to be entirely psychological not physical. And so the sons plan a party for the man, during the course of which they hide his crutches and tempt him to stand alone on the dance floor. As soon as he realizes he can walk alone, however, he runs out of the house, jumps into a car parked on the street and roars away.

We discover the 'key' to the parable when we begin to realize that the military vocabulary in the description of the man's second accident is *not* metaphorical:

> Am Mittag fuhr der Mann mit zwei Beisitzern im Nebel auf der breiten Autostrasse. Motor und Reifen nicht schonend, überholte er am laufenden Band und *triumphierte* bei jedem *Manöver*. Das ist gerechte Ordnung. Er war der *Sieger*, das sah jeder. Um fünf Minuten vor zwölf setzte er an, vier Lastwagen zu überlisten, die mit der Unerschütterlichkeit von *Panzern* ihre Strecke dampften. Als er den zweiten *besiegte*, bog der dritte links ein, der Mann versuchte, rechts vorbeizukommen und beachtete den vierten nicht: Kreischen, Krachen, Fauchen, endlich Rieseln wie von Regen, für Sekunden. Dann war es still.[14]

The man is clearly Germany and the accident is the Second World War. The trucks seem to be major nations, Poland,

---

[14] *Ibid.*, p. 74f.

France, Russia and the United States, perhaps even in that order, and he and his passengers are the Axis Powers.

Now we can see that the man's earlier accident had been the First World War:

> ... der brach in wenigen Jahren alle Verträge, die einzuhalten er mit seiner Unterschrift versprochen hatte, als ihm—nachdem er eines nie geklärten Unfalls wegen über ein Jahrzehnt auf die vier Räder hatte verzichten müssen—erneut der *Führer*schein [!] ausgehändigt und er in die Gemeinschaft derer wiederaufgenommen wurde, die am Verkehr teilnehmen dürfen; der glaubte, hinterm Steuerrad sitzend, die Welt gehöre ihm; der war Herr der Strassen, der hatte Macht.[15]

It also becomes clear why the two 'chief surgeons' who operate on the man after the accident—Britain and the USA?—"konnten sich mit den Assistenten nicht einigen;" and we realize what the "fremder Lebenssaft" must be—the Marshall Plan, etc.—which is 'pumped' into his body. The term "Wunder" applied to his physical recovery is obviously meant to be attached to the word "Wirtschafts-" and his father "Der Alte" can be none other than Konrad Adenauer. The photos of the dead are from the death camps.

But if most elements of the parable have become transparent, others are opaque, for at this point, only the mantic Anton Schmitz appears to understand the parable completely. We must follow the red threads of the allegory through the account of his subsequent actions, which make up the continuation of the parable, as it were, before we can hope to illuminate all facets of the story, especially those near the end which seem to take up the military vocabulary of the first part:

> Vielleicht begann Herrn Schmitzens Meinung über die Parabel erst sichtbar zu werden, als er mit seinem Hinketritt an der Theke entlang ging bis zum anderen Ende der Bierschwemme, dort sich drehte, zurückkam, wieder an der Theke entlang, dann an Peter und dem Kellner vorbei bis zur Ausgangstür marschierte, wo

---

[15] *Ibid.*, p. 74.

er auf dem Absatz kehrt machte, den Weg längs durch den Schlauch noch einmal abmass, zweimal noch, dreimal, wobei er zu tänzeln versuchte, zu schreiten, zu promenieren.[16]

Schmitz walks with a limp for he was wounded during the war, and when he limps around the barroom it is in obvious contraposition to this 'Man Who Had Forgotten How To Walk.' Schmitz had apparently wanted to determine if it were perhaps *he* who had forgotten, but, satisfied that it is not, he now begins to prophesy:

> Wir werden die Söhne des Mannes suchen, und wir werden sie so lange suchen, bis wir sie gefunden haben, und es wird uns nicht darauf ankommen, wieviele es sein werden, je mehr Söhne, desto besser; und die Söhne werden ihre Fahrräder von den Hacken in den Garagen stemmen oder sie leicht angerostet aus dem Keller tragen oder vom Dachboden und werden den Staub herunterblasen und Luft in die Reifen pumpen und Schrauben anziehen und prüfen, ob der Dynamo, sein Treibrad noch rotiert, ob die kleine Birne nicht durchgebrannt ist, dann werden sie ausfahren und werden die Töchter der Männer abholen, die ihre Geliebten sind oder ihre Freundinnen . . . . Und wenn alle beisammen sind, werden die Söhne und Töchter in gemischten Gruppen losfahren, und schon bei der ersten Wasserlache werden sie anhalten und das Auto, das da in einer Garageneinfahrt oder auf der Strasse zurechtgemacht wird, mit ihren Fahrrädern umstellen und zunächst schweigend dem Mann oder der Frau zusehen, die da in Schmierhose oder Schmutzmantel wie aztekische Tempelsklaven ihren Götzen abspritzen . . . . Danach werden die Söhne und Töchter in die Stadt radeln und sie werden versuchen, den Mann zu finden, der das Gehen verlernt hat, und gleichzeitig werden sie versuchen, den mit ihrem Gelächter zu verwirren, der zu laut hupt, oder zu oft . . . .[17]

Anton is interrupted before he can say much more by two elderly ladies who have come to have their daily cup of coffee. When the inebriated Scheel insults them, they leave in a huff but with Anton following, trying to apologize. Despite

---

[16] *Ibid.*, p. 90.
[17] *Ibid.*, p. 91ff.

the interruption, the essence of the fable—that there are sons and daughters who wish to reform their father(land)—has become a guiding tenet to Anton, just as the superficial vocabulary, the catch phrase 'sons and daughters' becomes a cue for the narrator, who picks up this cue again after much digression in a later chapter.

Anton's daughter Maria, as it happens, a pacifist and an 'Easter Marcher,' has heard her father's radio programs and hopes to win his support for the peace movement and for an upcoming demonstration on Good Friday. We are not surprised, even though she is, that he immediately accepts her proposal: to help her form a mass of bicyclists who would pedal through the city to the Neumarkt, the center of the demonstration. "Anton Schmitz erkannte den Vorschlag an als eigens für ihn ausgedachte Möglichkeit," says Johannes the narrator, thinking of the prophecy in the tavern. But Maria, who has not been privy to this revelation, cannot understand why "Schmitz aufstand und durchs Zimmer tänzelte und unablässig die Hände rieb, dass er sichtlich froh war, seinem Freunde zulächelte und dabei etwas murmelte, das sich anhörte wie: Söhne und Töchter."[18]

After witnessing Anton's reaction to the parable, we quite confidently infer that the sons and daughters of the 'Man Who Has Forgotten How To Walk' are the concerned young people of Germany who wish to see their father(land) freed from the crutches of his militant physicians and able to operate his own business. But when they arrange for him to walk again, he breaks away and drives off in the 'most powerful car of his time,' where the parable begins to repeat itself:

> Es war einmal ein Mann, der fuhr einen Wagen, der fuhr den stärksten Wagen seiner Zeit, der sass am Steuer und fuhr, der konnte nicht gehen, der hatte kein Ziel für seine Füsse, sein Ziel war das Fahren, darum fuhr er, der fühlte sich stark, der glaubte,

---

[18] *Ibid.*, p. 220.

hinterm Steuer sitzend, die Welt gehöre ihm, der war Herr der Strassen, der hatte Macht.[19]

The similarity of the words "Wagen" and "Waffen" cannot be coincidental, and that the man drives the most powerful automobile of his time quite certainly means that NATO-Germany (not to mention Warsaw-Pact Germany) again employs the most powerful and recent thermonuclear weaponry. Anton is quite correct when he judges that the logical sequel to the parable would be constituted in the attempts by the 'sons and daughters' to get their 'father' to give up his 'automobile' and begin to 'walk' or at least ride a bicycle, more humane and human forms of 'transportation.' He therefore welcomes the opportunity to be their leader in opposing the use of the most powerful weapon of his time, nuclear warheads.

III

Returning again briefly for reorientation to Peter Hay's paradigm of the fertile limping prophet, we now see that Anton Schmitz fits perfectly. His identity is certainly mythic, for he alternately plays the roles of *Adam* (stemming from his re-creation on that morning three weeks before carnival, during which his diet consisted of apples); *Jesus* (with his disciple *Peter* Scheel); *Tünnes* (short for Anton and referring to the Tünnes and Schäl—cf. Peter *Scheel*—of Cologne carnival folklore); and *Don Quixote*. Even his family name Schmitz (an extremely common family name in Cologne, we are repeatedly informed) marks him as a universal resident of that city or as a sort of everyman-figure.

On yet another mythic level, this novel can be viewed as a treatment of all German literature from 1945 on, with Anton Schmitz cast in the role of archetypal protagonist: the arche-

---

[19] *Ibid.*, p. 88f.

typal 'engaged,' limping, visionary fool. He is the 'Man Who Remembered How To Walk'—albeit with a limp—in obvious contraposition to the allegorical figure of the parable. As such he is the parabolical personification of that 'other Germany,' the father whose sons and daughters wear *Erkenntnisbrillen*, ride bicycles and oppose the arms race. This personification can perhaps be most clearly demonstrated by an examination of one more, strangely surrealistic, section of the novel:

Before the events of Good Friday and the demonstration, but after Anton has heard the parable in the tavern, Peter Scheel succeeds in temporarily luring his ward back to the broadcast house for a few days. But during a taping session Anton *apparently* takes leave of his senses once more. Anton has engaged a certain Pater Remigius Spohr to contribute to his series "Gedanken zur Zeit." The priest, sitting in front of a microphone in Studio 21, speaks to the topic "Der reduzierte Mensch." Anton and others are monitoring the speech in the control room when the door to the studio is slowly opened, admitting a rush of wind which rattles the pages of Remigius' manuscript:

> Da steht plötzlich ein Eingeschrumpfter im Studio, ein Däumling, so ein Vierkäsehoch und grinst, der Knirps, ein Gnom, ein Tragbarer, ein Zwerg mit einem dicken alten Kopf, mit viel zu weit bemessener Gesichtshaut, ein Menschlein, ein Reduzierter, steht plötzlich im Studio Einundzwanzig, trägt unter seinem kurzen Arm einen Haufen Zeitungen, alte Zeitungen, schmutzige, steht hinter dem Mönch und grinst und blickt dem Remigius in den Nacken.[20]

Although it is only Andres, the newspaper vendor, who has some kind of mysterious liaison with the priest, Anton the visionary literalist is struck by what seems to all of the others to be mere coincidence: this 'reduzierter Mensch' appears just as Spohr reads the words "der reduzierte Mensch." Schmitz

---

[20] *Ibid.*, p. 145.

runs into the studio and says to the dwarf "Sie sind eine Inkarnation, nicht wahr? Sie sind nicht wirklich, Sie sind ein Sammelsurium von Buchstaben." When the little man objects, Anton interrupts with "Nein, Sie sind eine Metapher."[21] Remigius begins to laugh when he finally makes the connection ("Stichwort Der reduzierte Mensch, meinen Sie das?"), but for Anton it is no laughing matter. He knows the power of a word.

And now the draught from the door again causes the pile of papers to flutter and a fourth person appears in the studio:

> Er kündigt sich an, er bildet sich soeben, aus den blubbernden Blättern am Boden entwickelt er sich, da werden Beine in Umrissen sichtbar und Arme, wie einer von fern her kommt und sich zu einer Figur verdichtet, so bildet sich da unten sein Leib. . . .[22]

This prone figure, seen only by Anton the seer, is a cripple "auf dem Weg zu seiner Mama." Anton speaks to him, attempts to make him comfortable by taking his crutches, rolling him over on the carpet and cushioning his head with Pater Remigius' jacket. The priest, the dwarf and all the people in the control booth are, of course, horrified, convinced that Anton has again lost his reason. He pays them no heed, devoting himself entirely to the moribund cripple. In an attempt to offer solace, he decides to have his own mother sent for so she can play the role of 'Mama' to the dying man. At his request Peter Scheel soon brings her into the studio and Schmitz says, "Schau nicht mich an, Mutter, sprich jetzt zu ihm, nimm seine Hand, streiche ihm das Haar aus der Stirn, *er ist dein Sohn*. . . . "[23] She is unable to see what he means so she merely stares at him like all the others. Anton now attempts to summon other helpers. He requests Remigius to invoke St. Francis, but the priest refuses. Anton then thinks "Falsch, der

---

[21] *Ibid.*, p. 147.
[22] *Ibid.*, p. 148.
[23] *Ibid.*, p. 151.

Gerufene, der uns vielleicht helfen könnte, müsste aus gleichem Stoff sein." Such a person occurs to him, and he says "Engelbert." When nothing happens he says "Engelbert Reineke," whereupon this character from Paul Schallück's previous novel immediately appears. But since even Engelbert seems unable to do anything for this dying man, as a last resort Anton requests Peter to call *his* name. "Sprich meinen Namen laut aus, Peter. Und Peter tut's zweimal, dreimal laut: Anton Schmitz! Keine Reaktion. Er liegt da und sieht aus, als stürbe er jetzt."[24] It is hopeless, Anton concludes, "er war zu lange unterwegs." The man dies and as the smell of death hangs heavily in the studio, Anton allows himself to be towed out of the room by Peter Scheel.

The correlation between this moribund cripple, a figment of Anton's imagination, and the limping Schmitz himself is subtly but distinctly drawn when he requests Peter to call the cripple by his name, Anton Schmitz. The 'Heimkehrer,' an archetypal representation of the postwar German protagonist, the cripple who was "zu lange weg" like a Wolfgang Borchert character[25] is finally dead, and the limping visionary fool survives as his heir. Small wonder then that Anton shows such concern for this 'Beckmann': It is at once his symbolical *alter ego* and predecessor, the postwar German literary protagonist par excellence. And whereas the 'Man Who Has Forgotten How To Walk,' the Beckmann-figure and Anton Schmitz all share the same infirmity, Anton succeeds both of them because he has been able to learn to walk again. His limp therefore remains emblematic of his essential nature, a reminder not only of his past wounds, but of his successful convalescence.

Thus he has chosen to call his feminine ideal 'Claudia'

---

[24] *Ibid.*, p. 152.
[25] A reference, perhaps, to the first lines of *Draussen vor der Tür*: "Ein Mann kommt nach Deutschland. Er war lange weg, der Mann. Sehr lange. Vielleicht zu lange!" (*Das Gesamtwerk*, p. 102).

not only as Johannes the narrator supposed ("anspielend selbstverständlich auf Colonia Claudia Ara Agrippinensis"), but because of the word's etymology: He seeks a *claudicant* Claudia.[26] Only such a woman could understand his attempts to heal, protect and disarm, or support his attempts to preach recovery to a crippled nation which has forgotten how to walk. With his claudicant queen, Anton Schmitz, like those other mantics Beckmann, Klaff, Schrella and Amsel/Brauxel, is the new (secular) 'Sacred King' of the old paradigm, through whose fertile, visionary leadership thousands of his 'sons and daughters,' now wearing their own *'Vatererkennungsbrillen'* can begin to see through facades, work to oppose the rearming of their fatherland and perhaps help make a moribund world fruitful and prosperous once more.

---

[26] Colonia Claudia . . . was the Roman name for Cologne. Claudicant means 'limping' from Latin *claudus* 'lame.' (Both terms refer to the historical Claudius, who was lame.)

Part Two
The Apocalyptic View of Certain Contemporary Phenomena

CHAPTER THREE

The Terrible Toys:
A View from Postwar German Literature at the Process of Play-Time Psychological Pre-Conditioning for Dictatorship, War and Holocaust

In a novel by Paul Schallück entitled *Engelbert Reineke* (1959)—mentioned briefly above—there is an important exchange between the protagonist Engelbert, who is an impoverished young high school teacher, and an evil industrialist by the (ironic) name of Paul Verlaine Sondermann. During the brown ages—the 12-year reign of national socialism—Sondermann had been instrumental in the denunciation and subsequent concentration-camp murder of Engelbert's father, Leopold, that eccentric (and admirably ingenious) antinazi humanist who eventually emerges as the actual hero of the work. Now, some years later, Engelbert is disturbed in his study of a book entitled *Hat die Stunde H geschlagen? Die wissenschaftlichen Tatsachen über die Wirkung der Wasserstoffbombe* when Sondermann drives up to visit his brother, Engelbert's neighbor (as well as the principal at his school). Apparently still true after all these years to his antisocial nature, he announces his arrival with a loud and lengthy honking of his automobile horn. As Engelbert watches from the window, Sondermann makes an exit from his vehicle (elsewhere described as "ein elegantes Reptil von blitzender Gepflegtheit") looking himself for all the world like a monster from some horror film: "Es schob sich, drängte, stöhnte und quetschte sich eine massige Existenz auf die Strasse . . . gröhlte lachend, während er watschelnd den Vorgarten stürmte."[1] His niece Hildegard (who in this thickening plot also happens to be Engelbert's girl friend) "wurde von den Greifern des Ungetüms umarmt und von dem Doggengesicht geküsst."[2]

A bit later, when Engelbert and Sondermann accidentally come face to face, Sondermann reveals he has learned from his brother that Engelbert is dissatisfied with his position at the school, and, like a cat with a mouse, sardonically offers Engelbert a lucrative job at his factory. During the war, Engelbert recalls, Sondermann had voluntarily switched his factory to the production of various kinds of armaments, including some types of mysteriously dangerous chemical agents, the reader is allowed to infer, like *Zyklon B*. "Wissen Sie eigentlich, was ich produziere?" he now asks Engelbert.

"Interessiert mich nicht."

"Sollte es aber, sollte es, wahrhaftig. Sie haben sich noch nicht danach erkundigt? Das wundert mich. Also: Spielzeug, junger Freund, seit eh und je Spielzeug für unsere Kleinen."[3] Doubtless still under the influence of the book on hydrogen bombs and now once again reminded of the deadly contribution of Sondermann & Co. to the war effort, Engelbert thinks he can very well envision the current production of such a toy factory, hence he blurts out sarcastically:

> Automatische Panzer und Düsenflugzeuge, kann ich mir vorstellen, mit Abwurfklappen und Zentimeter grossen Sprengbomben, die ein bisschen knallen, wenn man sie seinem Feind an den Kopf wirft, und Atomversuchsstationen auf Pappunterlage, hübsch bunt und handlich, und atomsichere Unterstände mit kleinen Krankenschwestern und verkohlten Atomleichen und Atompilzen zum Aufblasen, und Raketenabschussbasen . . . ?"[4]

---

[1] Paul Schallück, *Engelbert Reineke* (Frankfurt: Fischer, 1959), p. 28.
[2] *Ibid.*
[3] *Ibid.*, p. 33f.
[4] *Ibid.*, p. 34.

"Halt, halt, langsam," interrupts Sondermann, "das muss ich mir doch merken. Junger Mann, ich bin erstaunt, Sie sehen mich freudig überrascht. Sie haben ja Ideen. Sowas suche ich grade, einen Mann mit Ideen."[5]

Though the military toys listed by the sarcastic Engelbert are only a product of his hyperbolic imagination—whether Sondermann's factory actually produces such terrible toys is left unstated—the clear symbolic implication for Engelbert and for the reader nonetheless, is that Sondermann, this obese incarnation of the evil principle, is now producing (or is capable of producing)—in the subtle form of harmless children's playthings—agents potentially as dangerous in peacetime as those he produced in the war. This corpulent death figure and *diabolos ex machina* allows his mask to slip momentarily in his encounter with Engelbert so that his allegorically ambiguous words ("I've always produced playthings for our little ones") as well as the danger he represents to the present take on broader and more ominous symbolical overtones.

Like the apperceptive Johanna Fähmel in Heinrich Böll's *Billard um halb zehn* (also 1959) who shoots a Federal Cabinet member because she recognized him as "der Mörder meines Enkels,"[6] i.e., the potential murderer of future generations, the visionary Engelbert Reineke begins the otherwise rather unlikely perception of the toy maker as murderer. Gradually he perceives that the psychological training process for war, dictatorship and holocaust begins with children and can be accelerated and otherwise nurtured by the apparently harmless act of manufacturing, selling and promoting militaristic toys and games.

But these insights are not original with Schallück or Böll. Rather they seem to have their beginnings—like so much of

---

[5] *Ibid.*
[6] Heinrich Böll, *Billard um halb zehn*, p. 277.

postwar German literature, including the corpulent death-figure mentioned above—[7] in Wolfgang Borchert and in his expressions of fear that new generations of children might be trained for new wars by the same people, customs and institutions who had so insidiously trained his: "Nein, dafür haben die Toten ihr lebendiges, mütterliches Blut nicht in den nasskalten Schnee laufen lassen: Dass dieselben Studienräte ihre Kinder nun benäseln, die schon die Väter so brav für den Krieg präparierten."[8]

And, more specifically to the point of military toys and games, in the collection of Borchert's 'shortest stories' entitled *Lesebuchgeschichten*, one finds an instance where, to the horror of his more perceptive fellows, exactly such a pedagogue rolls a bowling ball down the alley at the pins, which look like toy men, all the while making little crosses on the paper as he keeps score, completely oblivious to the fact that the lethal results of his jingoistic sloganeering in the classroom exactly correspond to and are symbolized by the falling pins and growing number of crosses on the score sheet of his game. Another such Borchert story involves diplomats, also apparently oblivious to the portent, who stop at a shooting gallery on their way home from a peace conference to try their hand at yet another harmless game:

> Als die Friedenskonferenz zuende war, gingen die Minister durch die Stadt. Da kamen sie an einer Schiessbude vorbei. Mal schiessen, der Herr? riefen die Mädchen mit den roten Lippen. Da nahmen die Minister alle ein Gewehr und schossen auf kleine Männer aus Pappe.
> Mitten im Schiessen kam eine alte Frau und nahm ihnen die Gewehre weg. Als einer der Minister es wiederhaben wollte, gab sie ihm eine Ohrfeige.
> Es war eine Mutter.[9]

---

[7] See the gluttonous entrepreneur from *Draussen vor der Tür* in: Wolfgang Borchert, *Das Gesamtwerk*, p. 105.

[8] "Das ist unser Manifest," *Ibid.*, p. 313.

[9] Wolfgang Borchert, *Das Gesamtwerk* ('Bowling,' p. 316, 'Shooting,' p. 317).

Viewed from this symbolic perspective, then, the lines between toy weapons and real weapons, between war games and real war become blurred and the tanks, the guns, the planes and all the other military instruments of death and destruction begin to be seen serving in the 'game' of war the function of gigantic, ghastly toys in the hands of overgrown children, conditioned to their use from the cradle on. Thus Berthold Klaff, the visionary limping 'fool' of Martin Walser's novel *Ehen in Phillipsburg*, suffers from a highly significant nightmare involving a child's toy run lethally amok, after he is introduced to a young tank soldier who is for Klaff the very pre-programmed anthropomorphization of such a house-crushing armored vehicle:

> Und ging zwischen uns auf und ab, so schnell und mit so grossen Schritten, dass ich fürchtete, er werde die Wand durchbrechen, ins nächste Zimmer marschieren und auch dort noch die Wand durchbrechen und weitermarschieren durch alle Wohnungen der Häuserzeile. Nachts träumte ich von einer wildgewordenen Kindereisenbahn, die in tödlichem Tempo auf dem viel zu engen Schienenkreis herumjagt.[10]

Among the many other references in postwar German literature to such toys and games is one almost hermetic poem by Günter Grass entitled "Advent," wherein a child playing with his militaristic Christmas toys, and under the spiritual influence of some mysterious, evil toy manufacturer named 'Onkel Dagobert' (the German 'Uncle Scrooge' of Walt Disney's Donald Duck comic books) decides he and his friends Tick, Track and Trick (Huey, Dewey and Louie) "will declare a really spasmodic war on all parents and plan a communal family" (read: terrorist group) where evil is good and good is evil before going to school "in a 4-wheel drive Land Rover full of the neatest absolute guided missiles so that we can make the

---

[10] Martin Walser, *Ehen in Phillipsburg*, p. 198.

first strike." "If we are good," he says, "perhaps Onkel Dagobert will play doomsday with us."[11] And in Grass' novel *örtlich betäubt* (1969) one encounters an indefatigable old industrialist and former nazi general who fights and re-fights all the battles of World War Two in an electronically controlled sandbox with the avowed purpose of finding out why Germany lost the war (so that that injustice can be corrected).[12]

But there is one particular motif which can be said to be almost ubiquitous in postwar German literature as a symbol of such play-time pedagogical pre-conditioning for war, aggression and genocide, namely the game of *Schlagball*, a sport played very much like American baseball, with the notable exception that the runner is not tagged out but is actually hit—sometimes repeatedly—with the thrown leather ball. In Günter Grass' novel *Hundejahre* as well as in Böll's *Billard um halb zehn*—to mention only two examples—there occur almost identical *Schlagball* episodes. In each case there is a sinister coach/gym teacher (*Studienrat!*), invariably a zealous nazi, who, in order to "toughen the boys up for combat," is a tireless promoter of his party's cult of physical fitness, clean living and early rising, with special emphasis on racial doctrines of physical superiority.

Grass' sadistic *Studienrat*, the malevolent Mallenbrand, for whom *Schlagball* is a 'Weltanschauung,' a nationalistic, 'völkisch' alternative to the international and hence 'Jewish-communistic' game of soccer, is the author of a chapter on the subject in a book significantly entitled "deutsche Schüler-

---

[11] Günter Grass, *Gesammelte Gedichte* (Neuwied: Luchterhand, 1971), p. 179 f.

[12] Günter Grass, *örtlich betäubt* (Neuwied: Luchterhand, 1969), p. 141 f. Walter Kempowski, too, describes children playing at war games and singing "Wer will unter die Soldaten?/ Der muss haben ein Gewehr . . . ," a motif also found in Böll's *Billard um halb zehn*. One of the boys, however, is not allowed to play: "Erichs Vater ist Professor. Der hält nichts vom Soldatenspiel." Walter Kempowski, *Aus grosser Zeit* (Hamburg: Albrecht Knaus, 1978), p. 117 f, 67 f, 195.

*kampf*spiele." And in *his* games of *Schlagball cum Weltanschauung*—with specially lengthened baselines, as well as through previous collusion with his Hitler-Youth cronies—as a kind of symbolical 'sporting *prelude*' to pogroms and genocide, the hapless young 'Jew' Eduard Amsel is repeatedly and mercilessly victimized: "Schon nach wenigen Tagen regelrecht gespielter Weltanschauung blühten auf Amsels gesprenkeltem Fleisch mehrere blauschwarze Monde, die lange nachwelkten."[13]

In Böll the gym teacher is Bernhard Wakiera ('Ben Wackes'), his crony is the nefarious Nettlinger and their victim the young lamb-figure Schrella. Schrella's friend Robert tries —as does Amsel's protector Matern—after first running out some time on the game clock, to hit the ball high enough so that Schrella can reach the safety of home base. "Dreizehn Sekunden zu früh," he thinks to himself,

> wenn er jetzt schon schlüge, würde der nächste noch zum Schlag kommen, und Schrella, der oben am Mal auf Erlösung wartete, würde dann noch einmal losrennen müssen, und sie würden noch einmal Gelegenheit haben, ihm den Ball mit aller Kraft ins Gesicht, gegen die Beine zu werfen, die Nieren zu treffen.[14]

Imbued through his role as saviour to the lamb Schrella with a kind of superhuman strength, Robert hits the ball so hard that the opposing team is never able to find it—"der Ball, den Robert schlug" becomes legendary—and the game ends: "Er . . . hörte das Ah, das sich wie eine Wolke ausbreitete, anwuchs; er sah Schrella herangehumpelt kommen, langsam kam er, hatte gelbe Flecken im Gesicht, eine blutige Spur um die Nase. . ."[15]

First symbolically victimized in this game, Schrella is later beaten up by his schoolmates and then eventually

---

[13] Günter Grass, *Hundejahre*, p. 88f.
[14] Heinrich Böll, *Billard um halb zehn*, p. 33.
[15] *Ibid.*, p. 34.

caught by Wackes and Nettlinger during a nazi raid on his neighborhood and almost killed with a whip made of barbed wire. Only by stowing away on a barge bound for Holland and then by fleeing to England is he able to survive. Many years later, after his tormentors have become important, respected (and symbolically obese) leaders of postwar German society, Schrella returns from his exile, a limping, visionary ghost from the past, to warn the postwar world of the potential danger of their present 'games.'

In the aforementioned novel *Engelbert Reineke* the sport is not *Schlagball* but a boxing match, otherwise the motif is exactly the same, from the diabolical coach Gottfried 'Gott' Steltenkamp to the detail of the young nazi co-conspirator with the pernicious pedagogue, who in this novel is none other than Siegfried Sondermann, favorite nephew and most zealous disciple of Paul Verlaine Sondermann. After his bloody victory over the frail young Engelbert—naturally 'Gott' always badly mismatches the boxers—the old art teacher Lehmköster, who has secretly observed the match, looks at Engelbert's battered face and begins to prophesy in the manner of an Old Testament seer:

> So sieht nun ein Menschenantlitz aus, das tapfer gewesen ist. . . Die pöbelhafte Manier, sich gegenseitig das Gesicht blutig zu schlagen, erschreckt mich, sie widert mich an. . . Sie schlagen sich ins Gesicht, und sie haben Regeln erfunden, und Techniken, wie man die Kräfte des Körpers stählt und trainiert, um ergiebig treffen zu können. . . Aber schlimmer als der, der schlägt und geschlagen wird, ist der, der befiehlt, dass der Mensch auch im Spiel, auch im Sport den Menschen ins Gesicht schlägt. Und schlimmer wird es stehen mit dem Volke, wo solche Befehler angesehen sind und geehrt werden wie Fürsten, ob ihrer Befehle, und zu Führern berufen über das Volk . . . Darum ist der Zorn des Herrn ergrimmt über dieses Volk . . . und er reckt seine Hand aus über sie, und er schlägt sie, dass die Berge beben, und ihr Leichnam ist wie Kot auf den Gassen. . . und es wird sein, . . . dass die Städte wüste werden ohne Einwohner, und die Haüser ohne Leute, und das Feld ganz wüste liegt. . . Es sollen auch ihre Kinder vor ihren Augen

zerschmettert, ihre Häuser geplündert und ihre Weiber geschändet werden.[16]

Engelbert is amazed at these unusual words coming from the mild-mannered old man and concludes:

> Er war entrückt... Herr Lehmköster musste verrückt sein, nicht geistesschwach, vielmehr so geistesstark, wie es ihm natürlicherweise nicht zukommen konnte. Ein anderer sprach mit seinem Munde, vielleicht das Gegenwärtige, Immer-Gegenwärtige oder die Zeit selbst, geronnen in den Texten des Alten Testaments, dessen er sich nicht bediente, sondern das sich dieses Mannes bediente... Je länger er gesprochen hatte mit der wandellosen Stimme, um so mehr hatte die Maske Menschliches verlassen und Züge eines uralten, göttlichen, dämonischen—ich weiss es nicht besser—, jedenfalls Züge eines Wesens angenommen, das ich nicht kannte.[17]

The oracular words of this daemonic *Zeitgeist* speaking in Old Testament phrases through the mouth of Lehmköster form—from the postwar German literary point of view—a succinct paradigm of the genesis of holocaust and apocalypse:

> In the beginning there exists in the mob a certain aggressiveness, a willingness to hit and be hit, but it is without form and lacks direction.
>
> Therefore, rules, principles and instruments are created, developed and disseminated which enable one to hit harder and more effectively. Bodies are trained and strengthened for this purpose and the mind is imbued with the principles of heroism and courage.
>
> Simultaneously, leaders emerge, who order men to hit other men, first in an organized game, in the name of sport.
>
> Eventually, distinguished by their ability to give such orders, these respected and honored leaders are granted (military) rank as though they were nobility, until finally they become "*Führer*" of the people and catastrophe ensues.

---

[16] Paul Schallück, *Engelbert Reineke*, p. 137f. See Isaiah 5:25, 6:11 and 13:16.

[17] *Ibid.*, p. 138.

In the briefest of terms then, native aggression is nurtured and channelized into organized sports and games, then into the military and finally into the political 'arena.' Thus totally and lethally focused, the collective aggression of the mob is more than adequate to wreak total, apocalyptic destruction upon mankind.

And one of the most critical links in the infernal chain thus forged? "The manufacture and sale of martial toys and games, including the organization of *Kampfspiele*," we might expect our postwar German authors to argue, "for these represent the first organized step in the seemingly inexorable process of harnessing, cultivating and then unleashing mankind's basest and most heinous instincts." If the *circulus vitiosus* could be broken at that point, we might expect the German argument to continue, then the other steps and their consequences could perhaps be averted as well.

As if to lend realistic credence to what might otherwise be dismissed as 'metaphorical,' or as a mere poetic hypothesis, in October of 1978 then West German Federal Minister of Justice, Attorney General Dr. Hans-Jochen Vogel took a step clearly related to our theme: basing his actions on certain legal precedents in Sweden[18] he issued a strong appeal to German toy manufacturers, importers and retailers to refrain from selling war toys for the Christmas market. His initiative was supported by Federal Chancellor Helmut Schmidt who stated: "Gerade unsere Generation hat gegenüber den Jüngeren, die den Krieg nicht mehr erlebt haben, eine besondere Verantwortung."[19] And then, in April of 1979, in a significant test case which Attorney General Vogel followed very closely, the Supreme Court of the Federal Republic of Germany upheld

---

[18] See an article in *Die Zeit*, June 8, 1979, p. 2 and *Der Spiegel* of August 27, 1979, p. 153 ff.
[19] *Recht, Eine Information des Bundesministers der Justiz*, November 16, 1978. (Heinemannstr. 6, 5300 BONN 2, Germany)

the lower-court conviction of a certain toy manufacturer named Paulhans Handrick on the technicality of violating Paragraph 86a of the Criminal Code (that law forbidding the use of national socialist markings), by manufacturing and selling model tanks and airplanes adorned with swastikas.[20]

II

At this juncture, however, it might very well have begun to appear that these particular German (and to a certain extent, Swedish) concerns—literary *and* judicial—had assumed the form of a mild paranoia. It may have seemed that way at least to some Anglo-Saxon observers, whose homeland is the very cradle of modern sports, according to Johan Huizinga's *Homo Ludens*,[21] and to whose men of letters—particularly those in America—"possibly nothing is so common," writes Michael Roberts, "as homage to and yearning for athletic glory." Roberts also recalls what John Leonard wrote in the *New York Times*, namely that

> Hemingway, Fitzgerald, Malamud, Updike, Mailer and Roth, in short, American writers, go on promulgating the mysteries of sinew, the craftiness of give-and-go, safety blitz, double fault, power play, pick-off motion and betting the point spread . . . . Is this any

---

[20] Dr. Vogel was kind enough to send me many materials relating to his work on this matter, including a copy of this judgement, numbered 3 StR 89/79.

[21] "That the process started in 19th century England is understandable up to a point," writes Huizinga, "though how far the specifically Anglo-Saxon bent of mind can be deemed an efficient cause is less certain. But it cannot be doubted that the structure of English life had much to do with it. Local self-government encouraged the spirit of association and solidarity. The absence of obligatory military training favored the occasion for and the need of physical exercise. The peculiar form of education tended to work in the same direction, and finally, the geography of the country and the nature of the terrain, on the whole flat and, in the ubiquitous commons, offering the most perfect playing-fields that could be desired, were of the greatest importance. Thus England became the cradle and focus of modern sporting life." Johan Huizinga, *Homo Ludens* (New York: Harper & Row, 1970), p. 223.

way for grown-up writers to behave? Can one imagine Günter Grass [!], Albert Camus, Gabriel García Marquez and Kobo Abe similarly engaged as pompom girls? American writers care, morbidly, about the Red Sox and the Knicks. . . This is the culture of little boys who'd rather grow up to be a Pete Rose than a Gustave Flaubert; whose cathedrals are paved with astroturf.[22]

British subjects, too, might fail to see any harm in an athletic contest or the realism of a swastika on a model tank if their orientation toward war toys and games at all follows that of English authors like H. G. Wells, certainly no warmonger, yet whose book *Little Wars* has been the central impetus for and the standard work on games of miniaturized warfare since it appeared.[23] Played with toy soldiers, cannon, houses, etc., this kind of war game (including its more formalized subgenre *Kriegsspiel*—complete with its German title—which was and still is used to train British officers in tactics), was felt by Wells to have, if anything, the effect of making men and boys shun Great Wars, hence the addition to the end of his book of the apparently sincere but portentous pacifistic disclaimer (the year was 1913) that "you only have to play at Little Wars three or four times to realize just what a blundering thing Great War must be."[24] Two great and several smaller wars later, this sentiment was echoed by Isaac Asimov in his foreword to the second edition of Wells' book (1970) when he queried:

> Why can we not innocently play at it again in the fashion of an older day, and kill our plastic soldiers with wooden pellets, maneuvering them through a countryside of cardboard and harmlessly expend the aggressive passions we must somehow control? To replace war

---

[22] Michael Roberts, *Fans: How We Go Crazy Over Sports* (Washington: New Republic, 1976), p. 60f.

[23] See for example Donald F. Featherston's tribute to H. G. Wells in his book *Advanced War Games* (New Rochelle: Sportshelf, 1969), wherein even minor tactical concerns of the game—whether to roll one die or two dice—are couched in these terms: "For faster and bloodier battles an alternate rule can be agreed on." (p. 88)

[24] H. G. Wells, *Little Wars* (London: Arms and Armour Press, 1970), p. 100.

and perhaps, who knows, even do a micro-bit to prevent them, here is *Little Wars* again.[25]

As widespread as it is, this popular idea that war games "harmlessly expend aggressive passions" has not been substantiated by modern sociometrics. Recent studies cited by Eldon E. Snyder and Elmer Spreitzer in their book *Social Aspects of Sport* lead them to conclude instead that "the preponderance of evidence from . . . scientific studies indicates that [athletic] aggression tends to produce more aggression [in players *and* spectators] rather than serve as a catharsis for its release."[26] Likewise, Stephen D. Ward, a psychiatrist studying American athletes discovered that "A very common phantasy in a defeated football player is that he will meet his opposite number or the whole opposing team, singly or in groups, outside the dressing room and literally mutilate them in hand-to-hand combat."[27] The more involved with aggressive games one becomes, this research seems to suggest, the more violence is generated—rather than dissipated—and, as in the German paradigm above, one observes a gradual psychological transition from the realm of sports and games to that of mayhem and murder.

Any random search of the shelves in a physical education library does seem to hint at a connection—certainly a linguistic connection—between some athletic games and war, especially with respect to football: "Explosive Power for

---

[25] *Ibid.*, foreword.
[26] Eldon E. Snyder and Elmer Spreitzer, *Social Aspects of Sport* (Englewood Cliffs: Prentice-Hall, 1978), p. 135. See also Jeffrey Goldstein and Robert Arms, "Effects of Observing Athletic Contests on Hostility," *Sociometry* 34 (March, 1971), p. 83–90; A. Craig Fisher, *Psychology of Sport* (Palo Alto: Mayfield, 1976); and Richard G. Sipes, "War, Combative Sports, and Aggression: A Preliminary Causal Model of Cultural Patterning," in: M. A. Nettleship, *et al.*, eds., *War: Its Causes and Correlates* (The Hague: Mouton, 1975), pp. 749–756.
[27] As quoted by Robert H. Boyle, *Sport: Mirror of American Life* (Boston: Little, Brown, 1963), p. 63.

Championship Football," "Winning Football with the Blockbuster Defense," and "Football's Multiple Slot-T Attack." But one also finds "Blitz Basketball" for example, and there are sports even more overtly martial than these, as Michael Roberts reports:

> The refinement of promotional techniques in American team sports advanced to a new level in Spring 1974 with the creation of the . . . National Lacrosse League. Unabashedly and without mincing words the NLL appealed to the potential customer's enthusiasm for bloodshed—a historic point of departure. Predecessors in the industry had used violence—with varying degrees of subtlety—as a selling point but had never presented it as a game's *raison d'etre*. Never had a team 'sport' advertised by saying, 'Come on out and watch men mangle each other!'
>
> This, in so many words, was the NLL message. The Maryland franchise took the lead, with a campaign designed around a cartoon ogre named Crunch Crosscheck, whose motto was 'Ya gotta be mean ta play box lacrosse!' Along with Crunch's print ads, there were radio spots done as interviews with Attila the Hun (and Genghis Khan and Ivan the Terrible), who remarked on box lacrosse's striking similarity to the sacking of a city.
>
> At no point . . . were the NLL flacks accused of using hyperbole. Box lacrosse, already established commercially on a much smaller scale in Canada was the evolutionary perfection of standard (outdoor) lacrosse, a heinous pastime in its own right, descended from a paramilitary activity of North American Indian tribes. Historical accounts suggest its inventors used the game as a divertissement, as well as an amusing way to desecrate the severed head of a war captive, which was often the source of a ball.
>
> Considering both its antecedents and its public promises, the NLL had a lot to live up to. It didn't fail. After a first look, one observer wrote that the game combined 'the best features of outdoor field lacrosse with elements of basketball, hockey, soccer, and thermonuclear holocaust.' Another sportswriter said, 'Box lacrosse makes first-degree murder seem like a church outing.' Another was reminded of the 'battle of Stalingrad indoors.'
>
> Hockey, whose shining example had lighted the way for box lacrosse, catered to appetites for gore only slightly less brazenly throughout its half-century of existence. . .
>
> The National Football League, too, had exploited in not-so-oblique ways the fact that the game often had gruesome effects on players. There were commercials showing horrifying collisions, documentaries called 'The Violent World of . . .' There was an

ever-growing martial lexicon: blitz, bomb, trenches, suicide squad.[28]

To historical scholars, such things should come as no surprise, for historically, as Johan Huizinga points out in his standard work on games and play, "play is battle and battle is play."[29] This is evidenced already among the ancient Hebrews, Huizinga recalls, by an episode preceding a battle described in the Second Book of Samuel (2:14 ff) where Abner says to Joab: "Let the young men now arise and play before us. And there came twelve from each side [i.e. army] and they caught every one his fellow [i.e. opponent] by the head and thrust his sword into his fellow's side, so that they fell down together. And the place where they fell was henceforth called the field of the strong."[30]

Concerning Greece, where athletic contests and sports were most at home in the ancient world, most authorities agree that they were directly connected to and descended from war and fighting, hence they were even referred to by the more serious term αγόν (agón), as distinct from παιδιά (paidiá)—clearly implying 'child's play'—and the term αθύρω (athýro) 'sport of children,' or, in compounds, 'trifling, babbling.'[31] Whether in chariot racing, in the brutal, no-holds-barred παγκράτιον (pankrátion), in the javelin throw, the 'hoplite' race in full armor or in less-obviously martial contests like the long jump—itself originally designed to test a soldier's ability to cross ravines and streams quickly—or the discus (like the shot, a hurled stone weapon) the 'agonistic' quality of

---

[28] Michael Roberts, *Fans*, p. 145f.
[29] Johan Huizinga, *Homo Ludens*, p. 61.
[30] *Ibid.* (Huizinga specifically confirms for those of us with no Hebrew the correct translation of the word 'play').
[31] *Ibid.*, p. 48ff. See also the Liddell-Scott *Greek-English Lexicon* (Oxford: Clarendon, n.d.).

Greek sport was always paramount.[32] Even the word ἆθλος (*âthlos*), the source of the terms 'athletics' and 'athlete,' means "a contest, either in war or sport," which explains why it is used by Homer, for example, as a description of the Trojan war. That as such it is more than mere metaphor is further suggested by the adjectival form of the word ἄθλιος (*áthlios*) which, from meaning 'contesting' or 'struggle' came to denote 'miserable,' 'wretched.'[33]

The Romans, of course, adopted Greek athletics wholesale, as they did so many other aspects of Greek culture, apparently without making—in their term *ludus*—the fine linguistic distinctions the Greeks had between 'child's play' and serious 'agony.' That the Roman games tended toward the latter, however, with gladitorial fights-to-the-finish and chariot racing as in the film *Ben Hur* is clearly documented, along with the fact that drivers as young as thirteen not infrequently lost their lives on the *Circus Maximus*.[34]

With the exception of certain oriental war games like those "martial arts" practiced by the warrior caste of the Japanese Samurai, the most obvious heir to this Greco-Roman tradition of sanguinary sporting event is the medieval European tournament, which drew as well upon old Germanic battle rituals such as that described in the *Hildebrandslied*—themselves hearkening as far back as Abner and Boaz or David and Goliath—wherein a *champ*ion (cf. *Kampf*) was chosen from each opposing army to play a symbolical and portentous 'game,' or, as Huizinga formulated it, "an appropriate substitute for war, a concise proof, in agonistic form, of the superiority of one of the parties: Victory proves that the cause of the

---

[32] See H. A. Harris, *Sport in Greece and Rome* (London: Thames & Hudson, 1972), especially p. 20 ff.

[33] Liddell-Scott, *Greek-English Lexicon*. See also E. Norman Gardiner, *Athletics in the Ancient World* (Oxford: Clarendon, 1930), p. 1.

[34] H. A. Harris, *Sport in Greece and Rome*, especially p. 193 ff.

victors is favored by the gods, is therefore a just cause."[35] In addition to the joust, a tilt between two champions, a form of team jousting also existed, the German term for which is *Buhurt*, from Latin (via Old French) *hurtus*, 'thrust,' the source of English 'hurt.'

After the zenith of chivalry, and partially at the insistence of the church, which eventually came to condemn jousting as too brutal, mounted warriors spent the waning years of knighthood playing a game called *carrousel*, wherein they tilted from horseback at the painted forms of totem enemies mounted on a revolving mechanism. Later they mounted the mechanism itself (the ancestor, as the name implies, of our present-day merry-go-round) and tilted at some stationary target like a ring.

Several centuries later, when the rise of nationalism began to provide its great impetus to the renascence of things medieval; when the completion of half-finished and previously neglected Gothic cathedrals such as that in Cologne was finally undertaken; when medieval epics like the *Nibelungenlied* were being rediscovered; these paramilitary medieval sports too, were not overlooked, though their revival took a rather peculiar turn. In Germany, a book entitled *Die deutsche Turnkunst*, published in 1816 by Friedrich Ludwig Jahn (and Ernst Eiselen), documented the birth of a remarkable and widespread romantic cult, which was an eclectic agglomeration of fervent Napoleonic-era nationalism, militarism and physical education. This phenomenon, in nowise short-lived, lasted over a century and is distinguishable in an almost unbroken red thread leading directly to national socialism and to the chauvinistic gym teacher of postwar German literature.[36]

---

[35] Johan Huizinga, *Homo Ludens*, p. 113.
[36] See Michael Antonowytsch, "Friedrich Ludwig Jahn: Ein Beitrag zur Geschichte der Anfänge des deutschen Nationalismus," *Historische Studien* 230 (1933), pp. 20 ff and 80 ff.

And it was, in fact, though not readily recognizable as such on the surface, the direct heir apparent of the medieval and Greco-Roman martial games, an insight substantiated by the etymology of the word *turnen*. 'Turnvater Jahn' as he became known, coined this new German term for gymnastics as he says, from an old Germanic stem clearly identical to *Turnier*, 'tournament' or 'joust'. Hence a "Turner war bei den Alten ein junger Soldat," says Jahn,[37] "ein tummelhafter wacker Kerl, ein frischer junger Gesell, der sich in ritterlichen Thaten übete, daher Turnieren und ein Turnier seinen Namen und Anfang genommen."[38] His new exercises, wrote Jahn, have the same purpose as and are identical with

> Kriegsübungen, wenn auch ohne Gewehr, bilden männlichen Anstand, erwecken und beleben den Ordnungssinn, gewöhnen zur Folgsamkeit und zum Aufmerken, lehren den Einzelnen sich als Glied in ein grosses Ganze fügen. Eine wohlgeübte Kriegerschar ist ein Schauspiel von der höchsten Einheit der Kraft und des Willens. Jeder Turner soll zum Wehrmann reifen, ohne verdrillt zu werden.[39]

"Der Krieg ist nichts als die fortgesetzte Staatspolitik mit anderen Mitteln" the famous strategist Carl von Clausewitz had written at about the same time as Jahn's book appeared.[40] But war is also, he writes, "nichts als ein erweiterter Zweikampf, [und] wollen wir [ihn] uns . . . denken, so tun wir besser, uns zwei Ringende vorzustellen."[41] Thus it was a true son of both the nationalistic Jahn and the militaristic Clausewitz, Adolf Hitler, who decided to continue his political wars with other means, namely the means of ath-

---

[37] Jahn is ostensibly quoting a document of 1646 by a certain (suspiciously pseudonymous-sounding) 'Mannhold von Sittewald.'
[38] Friedrich Ludwig Jahn and Ernst Eiselen, *Die deutsche Turnkunst* (Berlin, 1816), p. xxxi.
[39] *Ibid.*, p. xvii.
[40] Carl von Clausewitz, *Vom Krieg* (Pfaffenhofen: Ilmgau, 1969), p. 27.
[41] *Ibid.*, p. 29.

letics, in the Garmisch-Partenkirchen and Berlin Olympics of 1936.

That Hitler misused the Olympics to further his martial and political ends was, and has been since, the subject of much outrage and spilled ink.[42] But to view the Olympic games as a kind of classical *sanctum sanctorum* first defiled by this modern barbarian is to neglect their 4,000 year-old origins and join their idealistic reorganizer Pierre de Coubertin in an illusion of a mere forty years. It may be more realistic to say that since Hitler, the Olympic games have merely started to shed some of this thin romantic veneer and have begun to reveal more of their true historical essence. From the bloody water polo game in Melbourne between the USSR and Hungary just three weeks after the Soviet invasion of November, 1956, to the black-power demonstrations in Mexico City in 1968 and the massacre in Munich in 1972, to the ever-widening boycotts of the games, first in Montreal in 1976 and then in Moscow in 1980, the chauvinistic and martial overtones of the 1936 games now begin to appear less the exception than the almost predictable rule.[43]

A direct comparison of the Berlin with, say, the Moscow Olympics may, of course, be unfair, for there are differences. But in fact, set over against the long-term and deadly serious ideological emphasis on sports by certain socialist nations today (not to mention those not always successful capitalistic responses to that emphasis), Adolf Hitler's political 'subversion' of the Olympics in 1936 now appears almost sportingly restrained. At first, to be sure, while the revolution was still

---

[42] See Judith Holmes, *Olympiad 1936, A Blaze of Glory for Hitler's Reich*, volume I of *Ballantine's Illustrated History of the Violent Century* (New York: Ballantine, 1971); and Hajo Bernett, *Sportpolitik im Dritten Reich* (Schorndorf bei Stuttgart: Karl Hoffmann, 1971).

[43] See Dick Schaap, ed., *An Illustrated History of the Olympics* (New York: Knopf, 1975), p. 282f.

relatively young, even the Soviet Union condemned such counterrevolutionary capitalistic games as the Olympics and refused to participate in them on the grounds that they "deflected the workers from the class struggle while training them for new imperialist wars."[44] "Bourgeois sport has one clearcut purpose," wrote Maxim Gorky for *Pravda* in 1928, "to make men even more stupid than they are . . . In bourgeois states, sport is employed to produce cannon fodder for imperialist wars."[45] But times change, and, as Henry W. Morton points out, by 1931 "the two basic aims of higher labor productivity and military preparedness had been combined in a mass physical fitness program appropriately called "Ready for Labor and Defense" (Russian abbreviation: GTO). "The GTO system," Morton continues, "contains such test categories (for all divisions and sexes) as grenade throwing for distance, rifle shooting for accuracy, cross-country skiing and the scaling of physical obstacles. Gliding, parachute jumping, and other "sports" having military value are greatly encouraged."[46]

Then, in about 1934, under the impact of the Five Year Plans and Stalin's strategy of "Socialism in One Country," the Soviet Union began to involve itself in international competition and to openly challenge its "young physical culturalists" to "become our new Masters of Sports who will surpass bourgeois sports records and will raise the banner of Soviet physical culture to new unprecedented heights."[47] During the coldwar era, finally, this policy has continued and, at least as far as the records go, has succeeded, as Morton indicates:

> The Soviets have made serious business out of sport competition. It has become a war without employing the tools of war, which is in

---

[44] V. P. Kozmina as quoted by James Riordan, *Sport in Soviet Society* (Cambridge: Cambridge University Press, 1977), p. 351.
[45] *Pravda*, August 14, 1928, as quoted by James Riordan, p. 351.
[46] Henry W. Morton, *Soviet Sport, Mirror of Soviet Society* (New York: Collier, 1963), p. 24f.
[47] *Ibid.*, p. 35.

essence the Soviet policy of 'peaceful coexistence'—not that sport nationalism was previously absent from international competition. But the Soviet strain is of a different and more virulent variety which has forged a direct propaganda link between sport triumphs on one hand and the viability of a social system on the other. As a result of the Soviet example other nations (particularly the United States, her ideological opponent, which had long taken for granted a goodly share of Olympic trophies) have been forced, willy nilly, to answer the totality of the Soviet sport challenge.[48]

At the same time, of course, the Soviets have retained the idea that sports in western countries are savagely militaristic. In his book entitled *American Sports in the Service of Reaction*, a certain A. Kuleshov brings us full circle to the world described by Michael Roberts *and* by the German literary paradigm:

> Special types of 'sports' and spectacles are organized in which viciousness and roughness reach their limit. The passions of the audience are whipped up in every possible way and the press and the radio savor the bloodiest moments in sports events. The blood spilled in the arena is to accustom the participants to the blood that will be spilled on the battle field of the contemplated imperialist war.[49]

III

One of the fine points not considered by Roberts or Kuleshov is that a game need not be as overtly sanguinary as football, boxing, hockey or lacrosse, or as overtly military as grenade throwing and rifle shooting, to be an important psychological or symbolical link in the chain of destruction postulated by the postwar German paradigm.[50] Indeed, it is the Soviets themselves who give us a major clue to this fact in the

---

[48] *Ibid.*, p. 82.
[49] As quoted by Henry W. Morton, p. 108f.
[50] It is one of the less-brutal sports—soccer—which in fact seems to be able to inflame the passions of spectators more than any other, and has even been given credit for touching off the famous 'Soccer War' between El Salvador and Honduras in 1969. See Michael Roberts, *Fans*, p. 33f.

attention and resources they lavish—paralleled only by that lavished on athletics—on a game so highly intellectual and rarified as to be at first glance the very antithesis of bloody strife: the ancient game of chess. In the Soviet Union, nevertheless, chess is one of the most important 'sports' sponsored by Ready for Labor and Defense and is given all the support and encouragement of an Olympic event. Recalling the genesis of this widespread Soviet interest, the "founding father" of Soviet chess A. F. Ilyin-Zhenevsky wrote of a military training meeting in 1920:

> Working with leading physical education experts on a programme of preconscription training, I proposed that the study of chess be included. I was prompted to put forward this proposal by noticing that when sport came under discussion it was valued not so much from the standpoint of its effects on physical well-being, as from the standpoint of its influence on the character. The chief value of sport, it was claimed, is that it develops in a man mental qualities which are of supreme importance in a soldier. Here a parallel with chess involuntarily suggested itself. After all, chess too—and in some ways even more than sport—develops in a man boldness, presence of mind, composure, a strong will and, most important . . . a sense of strategy. My proposal was accepted . . . Soon in our Vsevobuch magazine *K novoi armii*, I opened the first Soviet chess column.[51]

"We in the armed forces," Soviet Minister of Defense Marshal Malinovsky was to add in 1963, "value chess highly because it disciplines a man, helps to increase strength of will and powers of endurance, develops memory and quick-wittedness and teaches logical thinking—in a word it is, as the saying goes, a fine form of mental gymnastics."[52]

Though there is not complete agreement among historians of the game of chess as to the time and the exact place of its beginnings, in the words of Harry Golombek, "that it was

---

[51] As quoted by David John Richards, *Soviet Chess* (Oxford: Clarendon Press, 1965), p. 11.
[52] *Ibid.*, p. 28f.

in origin a war game . . . is quite certain."⁵³ Even the figures and rules of the chess board suggest its genesis: The king, for example, (Sanskrit *Raja*, Persian *Shah*) was seated on an elephant, the most powerful animal on the field, but, like any commanding monarch in war, he did not move about rapidly or in great leaps, hence in modern chess the king still moves only one square at a time. Originally, when the king was killed in battle (*Shah-mât*, 'the king is dead' cf. 'check-mate') the game ended, but, since this was later considered to be a form of lèse majesté or sedition, 'check-mate' came only to mean: the king is endangered, hence the game is over.

In art, the martial origins of chess are brought forcefully to mind by the American sculptor Roy Shifrin and his life-sized bronze entitled "Chess-Set," whose modernistic pawns are armed with submachine guns, whose king is a general, queen a woman guerrilla, bishops artillery, knights tanks and rooks computerized missile launchers, "ready to do battle," comments Golombek apocalyptically, "until the final check-mate."⁵⁴ But perhaps the most powerful artistic documentation of the game of chess as psychological and symbolical warfare brings us full circle again to German literature and to the nazi era. In his "Schachnovelle," written in late 1941, Stefan Zweig uses a game of chess between a few characters on an ocean liner isolated in the Atlantic as a microcosmic symbol, if not a direct allegory, of those international struggles which, at that same moment, were threatening the very existence of the planet. Though too complex to explore here in any detail, it can be demonstrated that in this miniature 'ship-of-fools' tableau the Anglo-American world is unified and personified in McConnor (that peculiarly 'American' rugged individualist

---

[53] Harry Golombek, *Chess: A History* (New York: G. P. Putnam's Sons, 1976), p. 14. See also H. J. R. Murray, *A History of Chess* (Oxford: Clarendon Press, 1913).
[54] Harry Golombek, p. 276 f.

of a Scotsman who made his fortune in California oil), whereas Dr. B. and in some ways the narrator, his *alter ego*, represent 'the old Europe.' The Grand Master and *idiot savant* on the other hand, the autistic Czentovich is, in this equation, despite his Slavic name, none other than the monomaniacal quintessence of the 'new Europe': fascism. In fact, in the microcosm, this imbecilic but eminently successful chess strategist seems to be an exact analog to that equally imbecilic but successful strategist in the macrocosm, Adolf Hitler.[55] All of the participants, especially Dr. B., perceive the game as a deadly struggle, a war of wits, resources and nerves. The Anglo-American McConnor is even willing to risk his entire fortune, if need be, to engage—more like a boxer than a chess player we are told—in battle with the champion. It remains for Dr. B., using tactics forced on him in the first place by the Gestapo to defeat the monomaniac.

But alas, his defeat is illusory and once again, the broken Dr. B., "von der Hitlerei heimtückisch überspielt"[56] like the diplomats and statesmen he mentions, continues his denouement toward certain disaster, either ending his own life as his exiled creator Stefan Zweig did (in Rio, the destination of this ocean liner, on February 22, 1942, one day after he mailed the newly completed "Schachnovelle" to his publishers and only a few hours after a final chess game with a friend)[57] or, at best, living a few more years, always haunted by the spectre of insanity. The continued triumph of nazism in any event, the ultimate victory of those monomaniacal autistic world

---

[55] In some ways Czentovich also resembles that most famous Grand-Master of chess Alexander Alekhine—Dr. B. does invoke his name in regard to Czentovich's play—an exiled Russian whose strong pro-nazi involvement during World War Two was used by Hitler for propaganda purposes against the Soviet Union.

[56] Stefan Zweig, *Meisternovellen* (Stuttgart: Deutscher Bücherbund, 1970), p. 372.

[57] D. A. Prater, *European of Yesterday, A Biography of Stefan Zweig* (Oxford: Clarendon Press, 1972), pp. 334–340.

champions of the games of war and genocide seems unavoidable.

IV

Granting that some kind of connection does seem to obtain between war, war games and war toys; between battle and violent athletic contests; between the strategy of war and such strategic exercises as chess; or even granting such a connection in the rhetorical realm—figure of speech, idiom, metaphor or simile—the question must be addressed as to why such connections arose in the first place and why they are so prevalent and durable. The question then, for the moment, is not so much: Is there a connection between games and war? but: If such exists, *why* does it exist?

Stefan Zweig, good Viennese that he was, doubtless would have directed us to look in the direction of psychology. And if he had known Huizinga's work (which was first published two years after Zweig's death) he, too, might have directed our attention to that phenomenon which all wars and all games share, namely a suspension of 'normal' rules of behavior in favor of a new set of *mores* specific to them:

> Inside the circle of the game the laws and customs of ordinary life no longer count. We are different and do things differently. This temporary abolition of the ordinary world is fully acknowledged in child-life, but it is no less evident in the great ceremonial games of savage societies. . . This temporary suspension of normal social life on account of the sacred play-season has numerous traces in the more advanced civilizations as well. Everything that pertains to saturnalia and carnival customs belongs to it . . .[58]

Similarly, speakers of German have attempted to explain the psychology of those crowds of people in 1914 who cheered wildly while troops marched off to battle with flowers in the

---

[58] Johan Huizinga, *Homo Ludens*, p. 31f.

muzzles of their guns by invoking the term 'schulfrei,' a word implying a certain puerile rejoicing at the sudden relaxation of normal and oppressive rules of cultured civilization in favor of the new freer rules of war.

Small wonder, then, that those crowds and soldiers in 1914 resemble nothing so much as athletic players and their spectators, whose behavior, Ralph Turner and Lewis Killian postulate in their "Emergent Theory of Collective Violence" is based on new "standards or norms that emerge [spontaneously] through interaction between participants."[59] A "consensus on appropriate conduct is established in the crowd," Stanley Milgram and Hans Toch further explain, "which then regulates the behavior of all, as demonstrated by the phenomenon of a buoyant chattering person wandering into a funeral service and quickly becoming quiet."[60] In situations like athletic contests, where normal rules have already been suspended, at least as far as the game itself is concerned, Snyder and Spreitzer likewise conclude that "collective behavior . . . develops through social norms, interaction and consensus that specifically apply to the situation at hand."[61] (The new and shifting behavioral norms of fans, of course, may not be exactly identical to those of the players, who are more rigidly governed by the technical rules of the game. Still, there is a great deal of continuity and flux in both directions between the two, with players often encouraged by the more 'un-ruly' fans to go far beyond the limits of the game rules.)

---

[59] Ralph H. Turner and Lewis M. Killian, *Collective Behavior* (Englewood Cliffs: Prentice-Hall, 1972), p. 21 ff.

[60] Stanley Milgram and Hans Toch, "Collective Behavior: Crowds and Social Movements," in: Gardner Lindzey and Elliot Aronson, eds., *The Handbook of Social Psychology*, volume IV (Reading, Mass.: Addison-Wesley, 1969), pp. 507–610.

[61] Eldon E. Snyder and Elmer Spreitzer, *Social Aspects of Sport*, p. 131 f. See also Michael D. Smith, "Sport and Collective Violence," in: Donald W. Ball and John Loy, eds., *Sport and Social Order: Contributions to the Sociology of Sport* (Reading, Mass.: Addison-Wesley, 1975), pp. 281–330.

In the case of hockey, to pick an example where a clear discrepancy between normal social rules and the rules of the game already obtains—imagine trying to enter an elevator under hockey rules—there also exists a discrepancy between what actually happens on the ice and what the rule book defines as legal hockey. In certain sports and games it would appear, in other words, that in the place of ethical or behavioral absolutes an ethical and behavioral relativism is created, a psychological Pandora's box opened and the skids greased for a slide from normal rules through special rules to no rules, a phenomenon perhaps better illuminated by the following case: In many games, but in one crucial contest in particular, a 16-year-old Canadian hockey player named Paul Smithers, the only black in his league, became the object of racial abuse from the opposing team and fans, especially from a certain player named Barrie Cobby. "It was not a hockey game," wrote sociologist Ross Thomas Runfola in the *New York Times*,[62] "they were waging war, a war orchestrated by a crowd that at times appeared to be emotionally deranged. The crowd reaction assumed an increasingly ugly character almost in perfect cadence to the illicit violence and racist baiting on the ice. . . At one point. . . the entire Applewood team and parents in the arena started to taunt Smithers and yell, 'Get the Nigger!'"

Because of this abuse and because Cobby had speared him with his stick, Smithers apparently decided to retaliate, but he waited (as Dr. Stephen D. Ward might have predicted from his studies of football players' phantasies) until after the game, accosting Cobby in the parking lot. During the scuffle, even though Smithers was restrained by other players, Cobby was kicked in the groin and he choked to death on his own vomit. "If Smithers' attack on Cobby had occurred during the

---

[62] Sunday, October 27, 1974, Section 5, p. 2.

game," Dr. Runfola continues in the *Times*, "Smithers would have been liable for a five-minute . . . penalty. Off the ice he was liable for a term in prison . . ." Convicted of manslaughter, Smithers was sentenced to a six-month term, but it was suspended. His lawyer told the *Washington Post* that, if he could, he would "close every arena and collect the hockey sticks and set fire to them. We're creating a stable of animals."[63]

The judge in the case counseled young Smithers not to give up hockey but to "learn to seek redress in a non-violent manner," a situation reminiscent of another of Wolfgang Borchert's primer stories: "Als der Krieg aus war, kam der Soldat nach Haus. Aber er hatte kein Brot. Da sah er einen, der hatte Brot. Den schlug er tot. Du darfst doch keinen totschlagen, sagte der Richter. Warum nicht, fragte der Soldat."[64] In these two cases, in the hockey arena and in the war, a young person has been 'schulfrei' and has learned to operate on a different system of rules. When he fails to shift back immediately and function normally in society again, he is adjudged a criminal. So too, those defendants convicted at Nürnberg for war crimes claimed that they were just following orders, i.e. rules of behavior. In their cases, after the primary system of (peacetime) rules had been replaced by the secondary (wartime) one, they began to operate on yet another system of rules, one established by the likes of Hitler, Himmler and Eichmann and which led to the extermination of millions of innocents.

In one of the most sensational experiments ever performed in the field of social psychology, Stanley Milgram asked volunteer subjects to be 'teachers' and administer 'electric shocks' to an actor posing as a 'learner,' thus recreating in a

---

[63] As quoted by Michael Roberts, *Fans*, p. 151.
[64] Wolfgang Borchert, *Das Gesamtwerk*, p. 317.

laboratory setting certain forms of inhuman behavior like that displayed by the Nürnberg defendants and other perpetrators of the holocaust. And although Milgram views the problem from the point of view of obedience to authority, his experimental findings also seem to confirm the validity of our theory of special rules.[65]

The accounts of the behavior of individual 'teachers' in Milgram's study make absolutely gripping reading. Among the minority (14 of 40 in the original experiment) who terminated the 'torture' before it reached the highest (lethal) levels there were people who displayed true heroism in defying the rules of the experiment. One such subject, a teacher of Old Testament liturgy at a major divinity school, as it happens, engaged the 'experimenter' in the following dialogue (interspersed with Milgram's comments):

> *Experimenter*: It's absolutely essential to the experiment that we continue.
> *Subject*: I understand that statement, but I don't understand why the experiment is placed above this person's life.
> *Experimenter*: There is no permanent tissue damage.
> *Subject*: Well, that's your opinion. If he doesn't want to continue, I'm taking orders from him.
> *Experimenter*: You have no other choice, sir, you must go on.
> *Subject*: If this were Russia maybe, but not in America.
>
> . . .
>
> *Subject* (spontaneously): Surely you've considered the ethics of this thing. (extremely agitated) Here he doesn't want to go on, and you think that the experiment is more important? Have you examined him? Do you know what his physical state is? Say this man had a weak heart (quivering voice).
> *Experimenter*: We know the machine, sir.
> *Subject*: But you don't know the man you're experimenting on . . . That's very risky (gulping and tremulous). What about the fear that man had? It's impossible for you to determine what effect that has on him . . . the fear that he himself is generat-

---

[65] Stanley Milgram, *Obedience to Authority, an Experimental View* (New York: Harper & Row, 1974).

> ing . . . But go ahead, you ask me questions; I'm not here to question you.

> He limits his questioning, first because he asserts he does not have a right to question, but one feels that he considers the experimenter too rigid and limited a technician to engage in intelligent dialogue. One notes further his spontaneous mention of ethics, raised in a didactic manner and deriving from his professional position as teacher of religion.
>
> . . .
>
> After explaining the true purpose of the experiment, the experimenter asks, 'What in your opinion is the most effective way of strengthening resistance to inhumane authority?' The subject answers, 'If one had as one's ultimate authority God, then it trivializes human authority.'[66]

This man acted in the way he did—I believe it can be confidently inferred—because he adheres to a primary system of values and behavior and does not allow himself to slip, even temporarily, into any other rule system.

Another subject, however, (whose behavior assumed bizarre overtones of sadism when he began to giggle uncontrollably at the 'victim's' screams) recounted in a questionnaire one year after the experiment:

> What appalled me was that I could possess this capacity for obedience and compliance to a central idea; i.e. the value of a memory experiment even after it became clear that continued adherence to [another] value, i.e. don't hurt someone else who is helpless and not hurting you [would be impossible]. As my wife said, 'You can call yourself Eichmann.' I hope I can deal more effectively with any future conflicts of values I encounter.[67]

Still another of the 'teachers,' who had been told offhand that the 'learner' had a heart condition, wrote the following reminiscence:

> I had about eight more levels to pull and he was really hysterical in there and he was going to get the police and what not. So I called

---

[66] *Ibid.*, p. 48f.
[67] *Ibid.*, p. 54.

the professor three times. And the third time he said: 'Just continue,' so I give him the next jolt. And then I don't hear no more answer from him, not a whimper or anything. I said 'Good God, he's dead; well, here we go, we'll finish him.' And I just continued all the way through to 450 volts.[68]

For our purposes it is significant that this subject, in reasoning about what he had done, mentions the problem of conflicting rule systems and his military training:

> This is all based on a man's principle in life, and how he was brought up and what goals he sets in life. How he wants to carry on things. I know that when I was in the service, [if I was told] 'You go over the hill, and we're going to attack,' we attack. If the lieutenant says, 'We're going to go on the firing range, you're going to crawl on your gut,' you're going to crawl on your gut. . . So I think it's all based on the way a man was brought up in his background.[69]

Finally the subject summarizes the experiment: "Well, I faithfully believed the man was dead until we opened the door. . . I did a job. . . I said to my wife, 'Well, here we are.' " When his wife replied: "Suppose the man was dead?" he concludes: "So he's dead. I did my job!"[70]

Since it was written with Auschwitz in mind and completed during the Vietnam conflict, it is not surprising that Milgram ends the book describing his experiment with a note on war: "The war proceeds; ordinary men act with cruelty and severity that makes the behavior of our experimental subjects appear as angel's play," he writes, before inserting into his book a *New York Times* transcript of a CBS interview with a participant in the My Lai massacre. A small portion of that transcript reads:

> Q. Why did you do it?
> A. Why did I do it? Because I felt like I was ordered to do it and because it seemed like that, at the time I felt like I was doing the

---

[68] *Ibid.*, p. 87.
[69] *Ibid.*, p. 88.
[70] *Ibid.*

right thing. So after I done it, I felt good, but later on that day, it was getting to me.
Q. You're married?
A. Right.
Q. Children?
A. Two.
Q. How old?
A. The boy is two and a half, and the little girl is a year and a half.
Q. Obviously the question comes to my mind. . . the father of two little kids like that. . . how can he shoot babies?
A. I didn't have the little girl. I just had the little boy at the time.
Q. Uh-huh. . . How do you shoot babies?
A. I don't know. It's just one of those things.
Q. How many people would you imagine were killed that day?
A. I'd say about three hundred and seventy.

. . .

Q. What did these civilians—particularly the women and children, the old men—what did they do? What did they say to you?
A. They weren't much saying to them. They [were] just being pushed and they were doing what they was told to do.
Q. They weren't begging and saying 'No. . .no,' or. . .
A. Right. They were begging and saying, 'No, no.' And the mothers was hugging their children, and. . . but they kept right on firing. Well, we kept right on firing. They was waving their arms and begging. . .[71]

If there are direct analogies between Milgram's experiment and war, they obtain also between his experiment and games. In both cases the new rules apply, and there is some kind of authority figure who insists that they be adhered to. In one case it was the superior officer, in another the experimenter, and, as a disenchanted former professional football player reminds us, it can also be the coach, the 'front office' and the fans:

> The Cardinals were playing the Pittsburgh Steelers in St. Louis one rainy, cold Sunday afternoon. We were beating them easily and then, with a minute or so to go, they scored. I was playing end on the kickoff return team and my assignment was to swing more than halfway across the field and block the third man from the kicker on

---

[71] *Ibid.*, p. 101 (*New York Times,* November 25, 1969).

the Pittsburgh team. I watched the flight of the ball as it went straight down the middle. Then I dropped back a few steps and began to sprint across the field. My man must have thought someone had blown their blocking assignment or maybe it was because he was a rookie, but whatever the reason, he was making a bad mistake: running full speed and not looking to either side. I knew he didn't see me and I decided to take him low. I gathered all my force and hit him. As I did, I heard his knee explode in my ear, a jagged, tearing sound of muscles and ligaments separating. The next thing I knew, time was called and he was writhing in pain on the field. They carried him off on a stretcher and I felt sorry—but at the same time I knew it was a tremendous block and that was what I got paid for.[72]

V

Despite all that has been said here about physical violence and aggression, the ultimate concern of those postwar German writers whose views on toys and games precipitated this discussion is less physical than metaphysical. One of their main concerns, for example, is psychopolitical. They fear for the survival of democracy and freedom, something which depends, they tell us, on a rather sophisticated mental process of differentiation and pluralistic compromise. Thus a major enemy of democracy and freedom is, in their eyes, an attitude of unthinking dualistic chauvinism leading to totalitarianism. So whereas some sports and games may engender more violent or 'un-ruly' behavior than others, to a certain extent, it could be argued, in all confrontation games—in chess, hockey, football, basketball, boxing, wrestling or tiddlywinks, as at Mauthausen and My Lai—the world tends to be simplified and reduced to the barest Manichean polarity: black vs. white, Cardinals vs. Steelers, 'us' vs. 'them,' Aryans vs. Jews, and GI's vs. gooks. Hence the first psychological seeds of such

---

[72] Dave Meggysey, *Out Of Their League* (Berkeley: Ramparts Press, 1970), p. 5f.

chauvinism, these Germans might argue, can be and often are sown (especially in young minds eager for simplistic explanations and for a cause to identify with and be loyal to) through sports and games. The immediate martial connection or violent component may vary: in Russia the process may begin with the GTO; in North Korea, with dramatic gymnastic stagings of heroic forays against the imperialist enemy (with wooden guns and bayonets against poster caricatures of Western leaders). In the West it might well begin with cowboys and Indians, GI Joe dolls, or when one school 'battles' against another, and the students of each are drilled—with banners, bands and other forms of military spectacle—to avow their undying loyalty to the team and the school, then, by extension, to the region, the city, state and country. (Consequently, high school football teams in Texas are described as defending the town against the aliens, or, in the words of a Baylor football coach: "The community expects a boy who's able to play to play. . . It's like feudal times and each town is a kingdom at war with the other. . .")[73]

In both the West and East, when this condition of dualistic hebetation has progressed far enough, it leaves the realm of games, and even major political meetings (partially perhaps because they are often staged in the psychologically associative environment of sporting arenas) begin to take on the character of battles between light and dark, good and evil. Rather than reasoning calmly together as men and women of goodwill who understand the complexities of a pluralistic society, often enough 'fans' of certain 'champions,' causes or regions line up along dualistic lines and allow 'fan-atical' (the source of the word 'fan') cheering and jeering to take the place of reasoned deliberation. And when this occurs, now as in the stadium at Nürnberg in 1934 or Berlin in 1936, the 'final score'

---

[73] Michael Roberts, *Fans*, p. 26n.

is again likely to read: Hawks 50,000, Doves 0. (Even as this book goes to press, certain attitudes in Britain and in Argentina seem to bear out this thesis once again.)

But what if they gave a war game and nobody came? What if society began to recognize more fully the subtle influence of play on behavior? What if it began to exchange its present games for those whose rules tend to reinforce, rather than undermine, the desirable *mores* of a peaceful democracy? It would appear that more and more persons, especially in Europe, have begun to feel the same about *Kampfspiele* and war toys as the postwar German writers cited above. Others may yet be persuaded by them and by the continuing efforts of jurists and politicians like Vogel and Schmidt. As for the United States, the growing number of sociological studies and other books[74] on related subjects—including whole series by publishers like Addison-Wesley or New Republic and an increasing number of exposés by athletes themselves—suggests increasing awareness here as well that sports fanaticism may have become a national problem. Videotaped and widely replayed athletic assaults like that on basketball player Rudi Tomjanovich (and his subsequent multimillion dollar damage settlement) or the dismissal of football coach Woody Hayes (who attacked a player on TV) have perhaps helped focus public attention, as have recent TV programs on violence in hockey and exploitation of student athletes.

In addition, many younger parents seem to have developed negative attitudes towards buying guns and other war toys for their children, in part perhaps as a spin-off from recent educational toy advertising which called their attention to the power of toys to mold young minds for good *or* ill. Then too, after Vietnam, after losing *our* unjust war, one for which *we* felt

---

[74] The largest bibliographies on the subject appear in Snyder and Spreitzer as well as in a first-rate book by Jay J. Coakley, *Sport in Society, Issues and Controversies* (St. Louis: C. V. Mosby, 1978).

responsible, we may have developed, more or less spontaneously, attitudes about war toys and war games analogous to that of the postwar Germans. This newer generation, with its innate suspicions of war toys, deadly serious competition for young children, dictatorial coaches and 'fan-atical' behavior at sporting events, appears, at any rate, to have begun to turn for its play more and more to games emphasizing the individual, where normal rules of behavior still apply and are even reinforced. In contrast to traditional 'technosport,' such games have been called 'ecosport,' something William Johnson in *Sports Illustrated* described as:

> natural play, unstructured, free blown. Its games are open, flowing, perhaps without boundaries, often without rules [i.e. *special* rules], usually without scoreboards, sometimes without end, middle or measurable victory. Everyone participates and the overriding slogan might well be, 'If a sport is worth playing, it is worth playing badly.'[75]

Noncombative, nonsymbolic, individualistic "ecosports" like backpacking, hiking, bicycling, frisbee throwing, jogging or ski touring have already begun to involve many Americans, and this trend away from 'them vs. us' sports shows no sign of weakening.

If this trend should continue, and if large, influential institutions such as schools, colleges and universities began to offer courses on sports and games in History, Sociology, Philosophy, etc., and began to de-emphasize both potentially violent competitive sports as well as the idea of *one* team symbolically representing the entire institution (as some have already begun to do as a result of pressure brought to bear on their athletic programs by Title-IX sex-discrimination legislation or by disgruntled students, faculty and alumni); if more well-known athletes were to 'defect' and 'tell all'; if citizens in

---

[75] William O. Johnson, "From Here to 2000," *Sports Illustrated* 41 (26), pp. 73–83.

Western and Eastern countries alike began systematically to withdraw support from the Olympic games unless they were freed from symbolic political and nationalistic burdens and martial events were eliminated; if organized religion began to speak out against excesses and abuses in sport (unlike current 'athletes in action' groups who seem to use sport as a lever for converting fans to their particular belief in the 'master coach');[76] if American writers shifted from their traditionally 'machismo' attitudes toward martial games; if the law-making and law-enforcement communities began to counteract ethical and behavioral relativism by prosecuting violent behavior within athletic arenas as well as without; and if these and many other similar changes were to be continued over a long period of time—then perhaps someday the human race, to paraphrase Isaiah, might not learn war anymore through its games. After all, the journey of a thousand miles begins with the first step, as another prophet, Lao-Tse, said.

I admitted earlier that some might find these ideas mildly paranoid. Yet according to Wolfgang Borchert, with whose prophetic vision it is perhaps fitting that this chapter close, people in all walks of life must begin to say NO to everything even remotely conducive to war, no matter how trivial, no matter how banal, no matter how paranoid in appearance.

> Denn wenn ihr nicht NEIN sagt, wenn IHR nicht nein sagt . . . dann: . . . eine schlammgraue dickbreiige bleierne Stille wird sich heranwälzen, gefrässig, wachsend, wird anwachsen in den Schulen und Universitäten und Schauspielhäusern, auf Sport- und Kinderspielplätzen, grausig und gierig, unaufhaltsam— . . .
> dann wird der letzte Mensch, mit zerfetzten Gedärmen und verpesteter Lunge, antwortlos und einsam unter der giftig glühenden Sonne und unter wankenden Gestirnen umherirren, einsam zwischen den unübersehbaren Massengräbern und den kalten Götzen der gigantischen betonklotzigen verödeten Städte, der letzte Mensch, dürr, wahnsinnig, lästernd, klagend—und seine

---

[76] See Jay J. Coakley, *Sport in Society*, p. 323.

furchtbare Klage: WARUM? wird ungehört in der Steppe verrinnen, durch die geborstenen Ruinen wehen, versickern im Schutt der Kirchen, gegen Hochbunker klatschen, in Blutlachen fallen, ungehört, antwortlos, letzter Tierschrei des letzten Tieres Mensch—all dieses wird eintreffen, morgen, morgen vielleicht, vielleicht heute nacht schon, vielleicht heute nacht, wenn—wenn—

    wenn ihr nicht NEIN sagt.[77]

---

[77] Wolfgang Borchert, "Dann gibt es nur eins!", *Das Gesamtwerk*, p. 318 ff.

CHAPTER FOUR

Reptiles and Robots:
Minacious Machinery and Its Automaton-Slaves

I

It will be recalled from chapter three that a key leitmotif for the monstrous Paul Verlaine Sondermann, the terrible toy manufacturer of Paul Schallück's *Engelbert Reineke*, is his black automobile, "ein elegantes Reptil von blitzender Gepflegtheit."[1] At first, of course, even Engelbert Reineke, until he finally dons the *Erkenntnisbrille* left behind by his murdered father Leopold, is slow to see the evil represented by Sondermann and by his car. In fact, he himself has applied for employment at the *Kondor* automobile factory, where he hopes not only to earn more money than he does teaching at Leopold Reineke's old school, but also to be free from the ghost of his father who was mysteriously denounced, sent to a concentration camp and murdered. After an experience at the *Kondor* works, however, depicted as an infernal region of flames populated by large, menacing, anthropomorphic machines, and after discovering his father's secret *Erkenntnisbrille*,[2]

---

[1] *Engelbert Reineke*, pp. 27, 35.
[2] Engelbert's interior *Erkenntnisbrille* has an unusual exterior manifestation: a stopped gold pocket watch previously owned by *(continued on page 94)*

Engelbert gradually begins to realize that it was Sondermann —another anthropomorphic machine and *diabolos ex machina* whose very words are bullets we are informed—who is responsible for Leopold's death.

For Engelbert then, the automobile had once been a symbol of the good life, the carefree industrial world into which he hoped to escape from the school. Seeing it now for the first time in its symbolical light, the seer barely resists the temptation to smash the windows in Paul's black car when he crosses the street in front of it. He has begun to comprehend that a car, too, can be a technological 'reptile' or 'condor,' a menacing device, always capable, like the 'most powerful automobile of his time' in Schallück's parable from *Don Quichotte in Köln*, of killing and maiming vulnerable human beings.[3]

For Engelbert the connection between aggression, the automobile, industrialization, war machines and nuclear weaponry is merely implicit in the book on hydrogen bombs he is reading when he first hears industrialist Sondermann arrogantly honking the horn of his car and conjectures about the production of Sondermann's toy factory. For Anton Schmitz, the Don Quixote of Cologne, it is explicit. From his parabolic point of view, any driver who 'honks too loudly or too often' is, like Paul Sondermann, an enemy of humanity, a 'Man Who Has Forgotten How To Walk' and an idolator worshipping his machine like an 'Aztec temple slave.'

This peculiarly technophobic outlook is shared by many of Heinrich Böll's secular seers as well. Father and Son Gruhl, for example, from the novel *Ende einer Dienstfahrt* (1966), decide to protest against the arms race and other manifestations

---

(continued from page 93) his mantic father Leopold, which seems to have a mind of its own, relaying messages to Engelbert about the dangers of industry and machines in general, and, more particularly, about the dangers of the archautomaton Paul Sondermann.
  [3] *Engelbert Reineke*, p. 119f.

of militarism in the Federal Republic by ritualistically burning a German-Army jeep as they stand nearby rhythmically clicking their pipes together and chanting the *Ora Pro Nobis*.[4] Alfred Schrella, of course, reacts toward Nettlinger and his symbolic limousine in much the same way Engelbert does toward Sondermann and his 'reptile.'[5] And in Grass' *Hundejahre*, the firm belonging to the mimetic mantic Amsel/Brauxel owns BMW limousines, the reader is carefully informed, a product of the Bavarian Motor Works, something closely associated in the popular mind (and no doubt in Grass' as well) with that patriotic Bavarian automobile and motorcycle-buff Franz Josef Strauss,[6] whose *alter ego* Onkel Dagobert in the poem "Advent" provides Huey, Dewey and Louie with a sophisticated weapons system based on a '4-wheel drive Land Rover.'[7]

Like Herman Hesse before them, whose novel *Der Steppenwolf* contains one dream-like sequence in the 'magic theater' entitled: "Auf zum fröhlichen Jagen! Hochjagd auf Automobile" (where "der Kampf zwischen Menschen und Maschinen, lang vorbereitet, lang erwartet, lang gefürchtet, nun endlich zum Ausbruch gekommen war"[8]), Grass, Böll, Schallück and others have employed the motor vehicle as a new symbol for an age-old phenomenon: the displacement of and disregard for the human individual in the interest of the machine. For them, the automobile is not only the Aztec god, it is the Procrustean Bed of the twentieth century. In the words of Lewis Mumford, it stands for all those scientific discoveries, technical advances and mechanistic world-views which have produced both the pyramids and the principle of *Gleichschaltung*; firearms, poison gas and regimented armies; industrial

---

[4] Heinrich Böll, *Ende einer Dienstfahrt* (Munich: DTV, 1969), p. 27.
[5] *Billard um halb zehn*, p. 145 ff.
[6] *Hundejahre*, p. 479
[7] See chapter three.
[8] *Der Steppenwolf*, p. 196ff.

wastelands and the hydrogen bomb. Killing or maiming over a million people in the world annually, the automobile is technology's own *reductio ad absurdum*.

As such, the automobile succeeds the traditional symbol of daemonic technology, the steam engine.[9] In his work on technology and the pastoral ideal in America,[10] Leo Marx discusses the traditional use of the steam engine by American writers as a symbol of all those forces which disturb the tranquility of the paradisaical American landscape, itself a symbol since Shakespeare's *Tempest* of the divine harmony between man and his organic universe. Although the pattern can ultimately be traced to the industrial revolution in England and to such expressions as Blake's "dark Satanic mills,"[11] the paradigmatic example cited by Marx concerns Nathaniel Hawthorne, who, on July 27, 1844, retired with his pen and paper to a pastoral setting near Concord, Massachusetts which he called 'Sleepy Hollow,' to "await such little events as may happen." For several pages he sets down random sensory images from nature, mingling these almost imperceptibly with harmonious sense impressions which have their origin in man and rural society. He continues to describe this state of being in which there is no tension between man and nature until his attention is suddenly shifted: "But hark! there is the whistle of the locomotive—the long shriek, harsh, above all other harshness." Marx demonstrates that this same motif, rendered here in its simplest form by Hawthorne, "appeared everywhere in American writing thereafter" by citing numerous other examples like the scene in *Huckleberry Finn* where a steamboat

---

[9] According to Lewis Mumford, the most archetypal 'power machine' is not the steam engine but the cannon, this rudimentary, one-cylinder, internal combustion engine, after which the first modern power engines were patterned. Lewis Mumford, *Technics and Civilization* (New York: Harcourt, Brace and World, 1934), p. 88.

[10] Leo Marx, *The Machine in the Garden* (New York: Oxford University Press, 1964).

[11] Exactly like Schallück's description of industrial plants.

suddenly emerges from the night to smash the raft upon which Huck and Jim are peacefully floating.[12] But although the paradigm remained essentially the same into the twentieth century, one small aspect does apparently change—the minacious steam engine becomes an automobile.

As a concluding example of his thesis Marx discusses Fitzgerald's *The Great Gatsby*; and he pays special attention to the narrator's description of the "valley of ashes" near Wilson's garage (and the all-seeing *Erkenntnisbrille* on the billboard?), which for Marx clearly constitutes the technological antithesis of the archetypal pastoral landscape. Near the valley of ashes the "motor road joins the railroad and runs beside it for a quarter of a mile," Fitzgerald wrote, as if to depict topographically the metamorphosis of the symbol:

> This is a valley of ashes—a fantastic farm where ashes grow like wheat into ridges and hills and grotesque gardens; where ashes take the forms of houses and chimneys and rising smoke and, finally, with a translucent effort, of ash-gray men who move dimly and already crumbling through the powdery air. Occasionally a line of gray cars crawls along an invisible track, gives out a ghastly creak, and comes to rest, and immediately the ash-gray men swarm up with leaden spades and stir up an impenetrable cloud, which screens their obscure operations from your sight.[13]

---

[12] Although outside the scope of Marx's book, one of the most interesting examples of the motif of the steam engine is Gerhart Hauptmann's story "Bahnwärter Thiel" (1887), which gives us some valuable insight not mentioned by Marx, into the genesis of the symbol. The imagery used by Hauptmann to describe the murderous train breaking into Thiel's holy sanctuary is equestrian. For Hauptmann, then, the train is the 'iron horse' which links up the steam engine with earlier, equestrian symbols of brute power like those in Goethe's *Egmont*, for example, or in Kafka's "Ein Landarzt." (Cf. L. A. Willoughby, "The Image of the Horse and Charioteer in Goethe's Poetry," *Publications of the English Goethe Society* XV (1946), pp. 47–70.) One other interesting aspect of Hauptmann's story is his portrayal of Thiel's second wife as she digs in the potato field. This humanoid machine, who functions together with the train to cause the death of little Tobias, is also described in terms of brute, animal power analogous to that of the horse. If the train is Hauptmann's symbol for minacious technology, this woman is its humanoid robot counterpart.

[13] F. Scott Fitzgerald, *The Great Gatsby* (New York: Charles Scribner's Sons, 1925), p. 23.

"This hideous, man-made wilderness is a product of the technological power that also makes possible Gatsby's wealth, his parties, his car," Marx writes. "None of his possessions sums up the quality of life to which he aspires as well as the car . . . . As it happens, the car proves to be a murder weapon and the instrument of Gatsby's undoing."[14] If the steam engine had originally turned the garden into a valley of ashes, Marx concludes, by 1925, the publication date of *Gatsby*, it had been joined or even succeeded by the automobile.

But it was not only in the garden, in the prescient expressions of American writers that the motor car was to become the symbol of technological power; at almost the same time, in the land where the automobile was invented, a mad teutonic Gatsby and his chauffeur—aptly named *Schreck*—were playing their own symbolic games of international rivalry in a supercharged Mercedes. Albert Speer recalls Hitler's boasts about his car and driver:

> Schreck war der beste Fahrer, den ich mir vorstellen kann und unser Kompressor machte 170. Wir fuhren immer sehr schnell . . . . Ein besonderer Spass war das Hetzen grosser Amerikaner. Immer hinterher, bis die der Ehrgeiz packte. Diese Amerikaner sind ja Dreck, verglichen mit einem Mercedes. Ihr Motor hielt das nicht aus, lief nach einiger Zeit sauer und sie mussten mit langem Gesicht am Strassenrand anhalten. Geschah ihnen Recht![15]

The importance of this idiotic game and the symbol was clear to Speer a few years later, after large portions of the world had become in fact 'a valley of ashes,' when he summarized his testimony, as Hitler's minister of armaments, for the Nürnberg tribunal:

> Das verbrecherische Geschehen dieser Jahre war nicht nur eine Folge der Persönlichkeit Hitlers. Das Ausmass dieser Verbrechen war gleichzeitig darauf zurückzuführen, dass Hitler sich als erster für ihre Vervielfachung der Mittel der Technik bedienen konnte.[16]

---

[14] *The Machine in the Garden*, p. 358.
[15] Albert Speer, *Erinnerungen* (Berlin: Propyläen, 1969), p. 48.
[16] *Ibid*, p. 522.

Although it may have come as a revelation to the repentant Speer, for some it was not surprising that in Hitler the symbol had come full circle, from cannon to steam engine to automobile to cannon, for as Mumford had written already in 1934,

> to look upon the horrors of modern warfare as the accidental result of a fundamentally innocent and peaceful technical development is to forget the elementary facts of the machine's history . . . . The army is in fact the ideal form toward which a purely mechanical system of industry must tend.[17]

II

The concern of the postwar Germans with the automobile as a symbol of technological minacity is ultimately predicated—as it was in the case of the related phenomenon of toys and games—on their concern for the psychological effect it can have on its driver-slave. At the wheel of every black Mercedes limousine or BMW or 'reptile' or 'condor' in their works, there is a Paul Sondermann or a 'Man Who Has Forgotten How To Walk,' whose being is not only symbolized but also literally shaped by his machine. In this sense, Albert Speer's testimony shows that Hitler, in addition to being the first to use the means of technology, was in fact himself totally 'robotized' by it.[18] This 'robotization' of man, depicted so clearly by Amsel's robot/scarecrows, is the ultimate step in a process which its opponents see beginning during the seventeenth century. Lewis Mumford makes an attempt to date its philosophical genesis when he writes:

> At the beginning of the seventeenth century, there were only scattered efforts of [mechanical] thought . . . . At the end, there existed a fully articulated philosophy of the universe, on purely

---

[17] *Technics and Civilization*, pp. 87–89.
[18] Ironically, nazi writers were quick to oppose the mechanization of life and pointed out that "Blut und Boden" were supposed to reverse the process.

mechanical lines, which served as a starting point for all the physical sciences and for further technical improvements: the mechanical *Weltbild* had come into existence.[19]

The popular symbol of this 'enlightened' *Weltbild* was not the cannon or the steam engine, which represent the will-to-power, but their complementary machine which, Mumford says,[20] represents the will-to-order: the clock[21] (something also reflected perhaps in Engelbert Reineke's rebellious pocket watch *cum Erkenntnisbrille*). One eighteenth-century reaction to this *Weltbild* and to its symbol, the clock, can be found in Friedrich Schiller[22] who recognized in the theories and symbols of his time the beginning of a complete and ominous shift toward the mechanization of the human being. In the sixth letter "Über die ästhetische Erziehung des Menschen" (1793) he laments the fact that in the century of the Enlightenment human life had begun to sink to the level of a "gemeine und grobe Mechanik," instead of rising to a "höheres animalisches Leben":

> Ewig nur an ein einzelnes kleines Bruchstück des Ganzen gefesselt, bildet sich der Mensch selbst nur als Bruchstück aus, ewig nur das eintönige Geräusch des Rades, das er umtreibt, im Ohre, entwickelt er nie die Harmonie seines Wesens, und anstatt die Menschheit in seiner Natur auszuprägen, wird er bloss zu einem Abdruck seines Geschäfts, seiner Wissenschaft.[23]

German romantic writers were also quick to sound the warning against the mechanization of man along with his

---

[19] *Technics and Civilization*, p. 46

[20] *Ibid.*

[21] Appropriately, the clock was one of the first items to be mass-produced using other machines and interchangeable parts. Techniques used in making clocks gradually found their way into all manufacturing.

[22] Leo Marx emphasizes the influence of Schiller on his biographer and translator Thomas Carlyle, the leader of the reaction against the dangers of technology in England and America. Cf. *The Machine in the Garden*, p. 169ff.

[23] Benno von Wiese, ed., *Schillers Werke* (Weimar: Böhlau, 1962), pp. 20, 323f.

universe. E. T. A. Hoffmann's tales "Der Sandmann" and "Die Automata," for example, depict the sinister nature of those clockwork machines—exact predecessors of Amsel's wind-up SA-men—which stand in symbolic contraposition to real human beings. (And whether or not Hoffmann saw the connection between cannons and clockwork detailed by Mumford, he began writing "Die Automata," his first such tale, just four weeks after he and the other citizens of Dresden had witnessed the massive cannonades between the automata of the retreating *Grande Armée* and those of the advancing allied 'war machine' in the fall and winter of 1813.[24])

If cause and effect in the perhaps fortuitous coincidence of these battles and Hoffmann's men-machines can only be a matter of conjecture, the Great War of a century later clearly prompted many twentieth-century writers to decry and condemn the same mechanization of man, as Karl Robert Mandelkow has shown in his "Orpheus und die Maschine": "Das Thema der Maschine rückt im Expressionismus von der Peripherie in das Zentrum der dichterischen Aussage," he wrote. "Die Maschine wird zum leidenschaftlich umkämpften Sinnbild eines die Menschen in sinnlose Mechanismen versklavenden Schicksals."[25]

In Georg Kaiser's *Gas* trilogy (1918–1919), in fulfillment of Schiller's prediction, workers become simply part of the machines they tend, degenerating into a large hand, eye or

---

[24] The supersession of the perfectly innocuous parlor robots which had been so popular throughout the eighteenth century by Hoffmann's heinous automata predates by a matter of only a few months the conception of a similar creature, one which was to become the most famous technological miscreation of all time: the monster of Mary W. Shelley's *Frankenstein, or the Modern Prometheus* (1818).

[25] Karl Robert Mandelkow, "Orpheus und die Maschine," *Euphorion*, 61 (1967), p. 110. Not all artists of the period, of course, saw in the machine a negative symbol. Just before the First World War, for example, the Italian Futurists looked forward to and called for the advent of their mechanical *Uomo Moltiplicato*, a kind of humanoid superman.

foot, depending on their function within the machine.[26] The process of machines forming men in their own image is described in more detail by Ernst Toller, whose play *Masse Mensch* (1919) contains the following lines:

> Maschinen pressen uns wie Vieh in Schlachthaus,
> Maschinen klemmen uns in Schraubstock,
> Maschinen hämmern unsre Leiber Tag für Tag
> Zu Nieten . . . Schrauben . . .
> Schrauben . . . drei Millimeter . . . Schrauben . . . fünf Millimeter,
> Dörren unsre Augen, lassen Hände uns verwesen
> Bei lebendigem Leibe . . . [27]

In the mouths of these workers, who are well on their way to becoming 'mechanized,' even syntax and grammar become mechanical. And in Toller's play *Die Maschinenstürmer* (1921), it is Albert, a man already literally becoming mechanical (he has a wooden arm, Toller casually reveals, and is possessed of the 'spirit of the machine') who, in this same mechanical language, prophesies the total dominion of his creator over its soulless humanoid subjects:

> RUFE: Sturm presst die Tür! Sturm und Maschinen im höllischen Bund!
> ALBERT (visionär): Hihuhaha . . . Ich aber sage euch, die Maschine ist nicht tot . . .
> Sie lebt! Sie lebt! . . . Ausstreckt sie die Pranken, Menschen umklammernd . . . Krallend die zackigen Finger ins blutende Herz . . . Hihuhaha . . . hihuhaha . . . Gen die umfriedeten Dörfer wälzen sich stampfende Heere . . . Hindorren die Gärten, verpestet vom schwefligen Hauch . . . Und es wachsen die steinernen Wüsten, die Kindermordenden, und es leitet ein grausames Uhrwerk die Menschen im freudlosen Takte . . . Ticktak der Morgen, ticktak der Mittag . . . Ticktak der Abend . . . Einer ist Arm,

---

[26] An idea also expressed by Karl Marx, that industry tends to use people like the tanners in Argentina, who kill an animal only for its hide. Cf. Lewis Mumford, *Technics and Civilization*, p. 146.

[27] Ernst Toller, *Prosa, Briefe, Dramen, Gedichte* (Hamburg: Rowohlt, 1961), p. 305f.

> Einer ist Bein . . . Einer ist Hirn . . . Und die Seele, die Seele . . . ist tot.
> ALLE (in magischer Andacht): Und die Seele, die Seele ist tot.
> RUF: Albert lacht! Albert ist besessen!
> RUF: Besessen vom Geist der Maschine![28]

Bertolt Brecht and Hermann Broch were among those who were to continue this theme and expand on it, applying it to the next World War. Brecht's play *Mann ist Mann* (1926), for example, anticipates the mechanization of man under Hitler: Because their fourth man has been identified by some hair lost during an attempt to rob an Indian pagoda, the other three members of a British machine gun company persuade Galy Gay, an Irish stevedore who has gone out to buy a fish for his wife, to don the other's uniform for roll call. When the fourth man, Jeraiah Jip, decides to remain on as the God of the Pagoda, the three lay a plan to change Galy Gay permanently into Jeraiah Jip, "denn . . . die Technik greift ein. Am Schraubstock und am laufenden Band ist der grosse Mensch und der kleine Mensch schon der Statur nach gleich."[29] During the lengthy 'machinations' which involve the illegal sale of an ersatz elephant named Billy Humph and the subsequent 'execution' of the 'criminal' Galy Gay, Widow Leokadja Begbick pronounces the following 'stage aside':

> Herr Bertolt Brecht behauptet: Mann ist Mann.
> Und das ist etwas, was jeder behaupten kann.
> Aber Herr Bertolt Brecht beweist auch dann
> Dass man mit einem Menschen beliebig viel machen kann.
> Hier wird heute abend ein Mensch wie ein Auto ummontiert
> Ohne dass er irgend etwas dabei verliert.
> Dem Mann wird menschlich nähergetreten
> Er wird mit Nachdruck, ohne Verdruss gebeten
> Sich dem Laufe der Welt schon anzupassen
> Und seinen Privatfisch schwimmen zu lassen.

---

[28] *Ibid*, p. 385.
[29] Bertolt Brecht, *Erste Stücke* II (Berlin: Suhrkamp, 1953), p. 235.

> Und wozu auch immer er umgebaut wird,
> In ihm hat man sich nicht geirrt.
> Man kann, wenn wir nicht über ihn wachen
> Ihn uns über Nacht auch zum Schlächter machen.
> Herr Bertolt Brecht hofft, Sie werden den Boden, auf dem Sie stehen
> Wie Schnee unter Ihren Füssen vergehen sehen
> Und werden schon merken bei dem Packer Galy Gay
> Dass das Leben auf Erden gefährlich sei.[30]

At the Berlin premiere of the play in 1931, Brecht tells us that "Die Soldaten und der Sergeant erschienen vermittels Stelzen und Drahtbügeln als besonders grosse und besonders breite Ungeheuer. Sie trugen Teilmasken und Riesenhände. Auch der Packer Galy Gay verwandelte sich ganz zuletzt in ein solches Ungeheuer."[31] Five years later Brecht explained why the innocuous stevedore who is taken apart and put back together like a car finally appears as a monster:

> Die Parabel 'Mann ist Mann' kann ohne grosse Mühe konkretisiert werden. Die Verwandlung des Kleinbürgers Galy Gay in eine 'menschliche Kampfmaschine' kann statt in Indien in Deutschland spielen. Die Sammlung der Armee zu Kilkoa kann in den Parteitag der NSDAP zu Nürnberg verwandelt werden. Die Stelle des Elephanten Billy Humph kann ein gestohlenes, nunmehr der SA gehörendes Privatauto einnehmen. Der Einbruch kann statt in den Tempel des Herrn Wang in den Laden eines jüdischen Trödlers erfolgen. Jip wurde dann als arischer Geschäftsteilhaber von dem Krämer angestellt. Das Verbot sichtbarer Beschädigung jüdischer Geschäfte wäre mit der Anwesenheit englischer Journalisten zu begründen.[32]

During the decade preceeding this obviously somewhat contrived, *a posteriori* 'concretization' of 1936, events had given the play's initial symbolic thrust more concrete, allegorical meaning. By then, the fears of Georg Kaiser and Ernst Toller had

---

[30] *Ibid.*, p. 229f.
[31] *Ibid.*, p. 316.
[32] *Ibid.*, p. 326f.

already begun to be realized in the ruthless rebuilding of men into human fighting machines by the 'machine' of nazism. This process, and the psychological implications which play such an important role in postwar German literature were investigated by Hermann Broch, in the last volume of his trilogy *Die Schlafwandler*. Completed in 1933, it deals with events of the last days of World War One, yet it clearly looks ahead to the same nazi 'robotization' as Brecht's play. The heroes of the first two volumes in the trilogy, Pasenow, 'the romantic' and Esch, 'the anarchist,' consistently flee from factories and railroads which they view as threats. But Huguenau, their heir, is the personification of *'Sachlichkeit'* and literally loves machinery, more specifically a printing press:

> Die Druckmaschine liebte er noch immer. Denn ein Mann, der zeitlebens von Maschinen erzeugte Waren verkauft hat, dem aber die Fabriken und die Maschinenbesitzer etwas im Range übergeordnetes und eigentlich unerreichbares sind, ein solcher Mann wird es sicherlich als besonderes Erlebnis empfinden, wenn er selber plötzlich Maschinenbesitzer geworden ist, und es mag wohl sein, dass sich dann in ihm jenes liebevolle Verhältnis zur Maschine herausbildet, wie man es bei Knaben und jungen Völkern fast immer findet, ein Verhältnis, das die Maschine heroisiert, und sie in die gehobene und freiere Ebene eigener Wünsche und mächtiger Heldtaten projiziert.[33]

In addition to this kind of relationship *to* the machine, Huguenau actually plays at being a machine himself. When the child Marguerite comes by, she and Huguenau "nahmen einander bei den Armen, warfen den Oberkörper taktmässig vor und zurück und skandierten die Bewegungen: 'Pum, pum.' "[34] During the revolution of 1918, while preparing to perform his most heinous and mechanical acts, Huguenau unconsciously wanders out to the printing press and sits down

---

[33] Hermann Broch, *Gesammelte Werke* I (Zürich: Rhein, 1933), p. 469f.
[34] *Ibid.*, p. 470.

before it, his rifle between his legs. In a scene replete with religious imagery, he worships the machine and is in turn inspired by the parole "Haissez les ennemis de la sainte religion" (the religion of materialism), to bring the machine-god a sacrifice. The subsequent murder of the religious mystic Esch and the rape of his wife—both performed by the same phallic extension of his mechanical ego—provide a grotesque sacramental offering to Huguenau's mechanical god.[35]

After such contributions to the 'myth of the machine'—the idea of rebuilding men into robots, the parabolical references to the Third Reich as the great machine which creates man in its own image, the psychological heroization and idolatrous deification of the machine by its humanoid subjects, etc.—and given the technological innovations of the Second World War and the postwar era—we begin to understand that the views held by our limping postwar seers may not be so mad after all. Even the mimetic productions of Amsel/Brauxel's subterranean robot factory, a partial, brief description of which fills the entire final portion of *Hundejahre* with almost unparalleled literary bedlam, are not the visions of delirium tremens or acute paranoia they would at first appear, but a rational, albeit symbolic, description of the hellish real world of our day: "Der Orkus ist oben!"

---

[35] *Ibid.*, p. 644.

CHAPTER FIVE
Ethics in Embryo:
Abortion and the Problem of Morality
in Postwar German Literature

I

When the American writer Richard Brautigan dedicates his "historical romance" *The Abortion* (1966)[1] with a note reading: "Frank: Come on in—read novel—it's on table in front room. I'll be back in about two hours. Richard," he seems to overestimate his work's profundity and/or fascination by about an hour. (Random sample: "If you get hung up on everybody else's hangups, then the whole world's going to be nothing more than one huge gallows. We kissed.") But there are writers for whom the subject of abortion represents a great deal more than a fad, or the obligatory happy ending to a soap-opera seduction story; and it is not an accident that many of these authors are Germans, of the postwar era.

For one thing, there is a rather long history of concern for the problem in earlier German literature and other art forms, including such examples as Frank Wedekind's *Frühlingserwachen* (1906), in which fourteen-year old Wendla Bergmann dies as a result of a clumsy abortion attempted by her mother

---

[1] Richard Brautigan, *The Abortion* (New York: Simon and Schuster, 1966).

and Dr. von Brausepulver; some of Käthe Kollwitz' expressionistic charcoals like the graphic "Paragraph 218"; morbid poems of Gottfried Benn including the one entitled "Curettage"; and undoubtedly many more works from the periods of Naturalism and Expressionism alone.[2] But even if the subject can be found in the most diverse works by the most diverse German artists of earlier periods, clearly defying *simple* attempts at classification, at the very least it can be said here that its treatment had always transcended the banal, setting forever the more serious tone to be followed by subsequent German artists.

In addition one also ought to remember the general moral climate at Germany's so-called 'Zero-Point'—1945: Deceived and deserted by *Führer*, fatherland, church and God, the formerly confident believing German had suddenly come to a full and actual realization of a condition variously known to philosophy as ethical nihilism or existentialism. In a manner of speaking, the reevaluation of all values called for by Nietzsche had been accomplished by 1945—if not in the way he intended. Now *all* value-systems were suspect, and the more absolute the value the more suspect. In addition, the battle- and concentration-camp-scarred German was denied the mercifully naive Nietzschean vision of a realm beyond good and evil; his realm had been totally beyond good but he had experienced evil and knew its insurmountability firsthand.

This then is the ethical dilemma of a people which has literally been to hell and back: They know there is a hell, but they fear there may be no heaven. The postwar German knows there is wrong, for he has experienced absolute wrong. Absolute right, however, must be disallowed, especially since

---

[2] Cf. for example, Stefan Zweig's novella "Der Amokläufer" (1922); Friedrich Wolf's drama *Cyankali*, § *218* (1922); and Arnold Zweig's novel *Junge Frau von 1914* (1931).

conventional systems of absolute right have too often been the camouflage for their diabolical opposites. Their very existence, he feels, has eroded and then destroyed individual moral initiative, making their followers gullible, rather than ethical, more capable of blind obedience than of moral discrimination. The task, then, that was to occupy Germany from 1945 to the present, has been to synthesize, if possible, a new morality—individual, personal, anti-authoritarian in nature—by measuring all aspects of life, all deeds and all thoughts, against the recent experience with absolute evil.

In a very real sense, all forms of the shibboleth, *Vergangenheitsbewältigung,* this much-discussed postwar German desire to come to grips with the past, represent just such existential attempts to synthesize a new ethic from the few tangible, if negative, moral data provided by recent experience: killing is wrong, lying is wrong, aggression is wrong, blind obedience to external systems, myths or idols is wrong, all forms of dehumanization are wrong. In the pragmatic postwar ethic constructed on this basis, the external "thou shalt not kill" of its obvious traditional counterpart, the decalogue, is replaced by an internal, spontaneous individual statement: "It has been shown that killing or anything like it is not good." Such statements would, it was hoped, amount to a defacto morality, which would be essentially democratic or particular in origin, even though no guarantees were made for its potential. Such an ethic—it must be remembered—having no systematic competitors, since its obvious traditional counterparts had lost their credibility entirely, would need only to be better than its sole possible rival: nihilism.

Perhaps the entire process could best be described by the metaphor of postwar man ascending his own interior, mnemonic Mount Sinai to receive his own law at the hands of the only trustworthy lawgiver: his own heart. Instead of being etched in stone, the new law, this ethical corollary of the spontaneous cry: 'never again,' is etched into the collective consciousness and memory of man. Poets and other visionaries, the wise madmen, clowns and other limping seers of postwar Germany, more like modern-day Jacobs than Moseses, lamed, and at the same time exalted and inspired by their existential battle with God, become the secular prophets of the new ethic, teaching their fellows through their engaged art as well as through their personal and political involvement, to hearken to their own interior voices (and *Erkenntnisbrillen*) and to recognize and shun evil in all its forms. One of these forms is abortion.

Now that this process has been abstractly sketched, it would appear desirable to examine the—perhaps more convincing—concrete artistic models which have been provided. The first occurs in Paul Schallück's novel of 1951, significantly entitled *Wenn man aufhören könnte zu lügen*, set in the rubble milieu of postwar Cologne. The characters are Thomas Abbt, a limping veteran, and Marion Vaihinger, both university students, who have met and fallen in love. However, Marion tells Thomas that she cannot see him on certain nights of the week. When Thomas investigates, he discovers that there is a shiny black Mercedes parked in front of her house on those nights. In response to his queries, Marion finally admits that she has a liaison with a wealthy carpet merchant who supports both her and her alcoholic mother in return for her favors. Thomas insists that they can get by without the carpet dealer if he works in his stepfather's small furniture shop during vacations and if they can both get scholarships. Marion agrees to try, but the attempt is unsuccessful. Thomas is unable to extract an advance from his parsimonious stepfather; and Marion's pandering mother, who has inebriate visions of a wealthy match for her daughter, uses her influence to gain entrance for the merchant. When Thomas returns from a working vacation, he notices that Marion has changed. She refuses to tell him what it is that has changed her, but she promises that the condition will only last 'one more day.'

Thomas leaves her at her apartment and wanders aimlessly about the debris-strewn city—which is being cleared by means of a small train operating on temporary tracks in the street—until he is suddenly frightened by a 'phantom,' a deranged woman with a boy, standing on the tracks, who mutters "Ich wusste, dass du kommen würdest. Aber du kommst zu spät. Du hättest mich nicht allein lassen sollen." Standing transfixed on the tracks, Thomas narrowly escapes being run over by the "Schuttbahn" but then he dashes madly back to Marion's apartment, discovers from a roommate that she has gone to the "Gerbergasse" to get an abortion and runs wildly after her, horrible images flashing through his mind: "Marion, winzig, eine Puppe, auf einem zimmergrossen Tisch, davor riesenhaft, vertrocknet, eine Hökerin mit blutigen Stricknadelfingern, scharf wie Mistgabeln." Searching through the endless proletarian filth and chaos of the "Gerbergasse"— "durch Windelgestank und Kohlgeruch, durch entblätterte Flure, über feuchte Matten, stupsnäsige Bälger anstossend, von seilchenspringenden Mädchen ausgelacht, schwasige Küchen, ungelüftete Schlafzimmer, . . . gröhlende Stimmen aus besoffenen Kehlen und verschleimten Hälsen. . . . "— Thomas manages to find, in this "entblösste Stelle elementaren Daseins," an iron door, which is slowly opened to reveal the spongy face of a one-eyed eunuch. Forcing the door wide open, Thomas discovers Marion, who has been waiting for the abortionist to return. They slowly go home together, but Thomas' brain races on, the events of the day zigzagging through his mind:

> . . . zwei Pfähle im Bewusstsein, die beiden Schienensteher, das plinkernde Auge im Eunuchengesicht, man kann es ja wegmachen lassen, keiner merkt es, du sollst nicht töten, wer sagt das, nicht töten, was heisst das, los, Feuer, auf die Köpfe, Maschinengewehr hinterm Strauch, taktaktak tak, tak, alles Bauchschüsse, werden schon aufhören zu schreien, tak, tak tak tak tak, du sollst nicht töten, zum Lachen, das Herz hört man erst im Bunker wieder schlagen, tak und tak, wenn die Kerzen flackern, Gewissen zer-

hackt vom Maschinengewehr, Erziehung, Anstand, Menschenliebe—Restbestände, winzige Trümmerteilchen des Gewissens zucken im Takt der Kinderseele: Fünftes Gebot, du sollst nicht töten, also ihr nach, in die Gerbergasse, ohne Verstand, denn die einen streiten, Lebensbeginn erst bei Austritt aus dem Mutterleib, die anderen, gleich nach der Zeugung, die dritten legen Veto ein und erfinden die Wasserstoffbombe, aber das geschieht ausserhalb des Herzens, nach Gesetzen der Dynamik, eines verrückten Minuteneinfalls, das Herz schlug in der Gerbergasse, bis hinter die Eisentür des Eunuchen, warum, um in neun Monaten Säuglingsgeschrei zu hören, Studium aufgeben, arbeiten, Familie ernähren, Hosenträger verkaufen, sie hätte ein wenig geschrien unter der Stricknadel, wäre nach Haus gegangen, hätte sich ins Bett gelegt . . . aber,—so können wir nicht anfangen, Marion—phantasierte einer und raste in die Gerbergasse, über einen Mord springt keiner hinweg, Herrgott nochmal, Phrasen, anerzogen, angelernt, angelesen, Gesellschaftsimpfungen, das Herz schweigt zu allem, das ist es, hör hin, es schweigt, drinnen ist nichts, kein Massstab, keine Stimme, kein Zeichen, Leere, alles ist draussen, Paragraph 218 und die Gefängniszelle, Verbote, Gesetze, Verbrechen, Laster, Vorbilder, Nächstenliebe, Ehrfurcht vor dem Leben, ewige Seligkeit, alles draussen, der niedergeknüppelte Neger in New Orleans, Gehirn fliesst in die Gosse, Pater Lombardis Liebespredigt, die verreckenden Volksfeinde in Sibirien, moralische Aufrüstung in Caux, draussen, Ethik der Philosophen, draussen, griechische Heiterkeit, Tao, Nirwana, alles draussen, selbst Christus starb draussen, drinnen ist das Nichts. Abtreibung oder nicht, es lässt sich nicht entscheiden, so lange drinnen die Leere steht . . . [3]

The skill with which a very young author paints all the scenes of this early sketch is impressive, including that of the two shell-shocked refugees, for example, who in Thomas' visionary mind assume the role of Marion and the unborn child in some future Dantesque reunion in a hell complete with images from an infernal dwarf-train driven by robot-like demons with wide-open jaws down to the expletive: "verdammtnochmal"; but it is this last, intensified stream-of-consciousness section after Thomas had rescued Marion, where all of the previous images recur, which is the most

---

[3] Paul Schallück, *Wenn man aufhören könnte zu lügen* (Opladen: Middelhauve, 1951), p. 137 ff.

revealing. Filtered through Thomas Abbt's keenly sensitive visionary consciousness, the seemingly disparate, individual, fragmented elements of his experience fall into significantly associative juxtaposition: Mental images concerning the abortion evoke memories of Thomas' war experiences as a machine gunner, for example, which in turn evoke thoughts on the racial murder of a black, the liquidation of undesirables in Siberia, and, most horrible of all, the dispassionate development and deployment of thermonuclear bombs, thereby concatenating all such events. Feticide, the first link in the chain thus forged, is also its lowest common denominator—killing in its most primal form. Anyone who can kill a fetus can kill him- or herself, other humans or the whole human race. And, as we shall see shortly, he can also murder God.

Exterior, cerebral, logical arguments about whether or not abortion should be classified as murder are dwarfed by the cumulatively significant grouping of these interior images, by the suggestion that the machine guns are more deadly when they fire at their enemies' bellies, for example (even as they riddle but cannot destroy the conscience of the man who fires them), and by the sympathetic beating of these same conscience-fragments and the heart in time with the fetal soul. The heart becomes, in the last analysis, the central image of the entire passage, the interior measuring stick, par excellence, which beats all the way into the Gerbergasse, ignoring sophistical exterior, cerebral arguments *for* abortion (the very poverty, squalor and overcrowding of the Gerbergasse itself make it in fact a living example, a teeming reification of such arguments) filling with its higher, sympathetic beating the existential void. 'To have an abortion or not,' Thomas concludes, 'it can't be decided, as long as nothingness fills your insides'. But when this young protagonist 'learns to stop lying' and finds within himself, in his heart, the means, however meager, to decide about the death of the unborn child, he finds that he himself can begin to live again, even as Marion subsequently commits suicide by jumping from a bridge precisely because she cannot find these means. Just as this affirmation of his own life grows from his confrontation with death, then, a positive moral ethic has begun growing from Thomas' confrontation with evil, with abortions, machine guns, concentration camps, euthanasia and Hiroshima.

II

Six years after Schallück, in *his* first major novel, *Ehen in Phillipsburg*, Martin Walser treats the same subject. As in Schallück, a young couple, Hans Beumann and Anne Volkmann, confront the reality of an undesired pregnancy. Anne, a loyal, loving character, suggests the simplest and most logical solution: marriage. (And lest anyone suspect that she stood to gain anything by such a marriage, Walser carefully arranges the motivational factors otherwise: *she* is the highly desirable daughter of a rich industrialist, Hans is a nobody, an unemployed journalist with lofty social aspirations.) But—even though he himself was illegitimate and owes his very life to the fact that his mother refused to lower herself to pay the lewd 'price' of a goatish old abortionist—Beumann convinces Anne that *she* should have an abortion, glibly arguing that a forced marriage would cause later difficulties, that it would be a form of unceasing penance, that it would become a prison for a man who can only live knowing he had freely chosen his own course in life, etc. Unlike Thomas Abbt, this protagonist is an anti-hero, well on the way to becoming a despicable hypocrite and murderer—in fact the entire novel is clearly a reverse *Bildungsroman*—and the abortion scene is a major station along his downward path. This particular scene culminates in the office of a horse-doctor abortionist, who, after trying everything else in his bag of tricks, eventually decides he must operate. 'Anne was strapped down,' we read:

Die Frau des Arztes gab ihr Spritzen. Dann begann der Arzt die Frucht herauszuschneiden. Anne schrie. Die Betäubung wirkte nicht. Der Arzt sagte: 'Das kommt gleich. Wir haben Ihnen eine schicke Narkose gegeben.' Er trug jetzt eine dunkle Gummischürze. Drei Stunden schnitt und riss er mit Messern und Zangen in ihr herum, förderte blutige Fleischstücke zutage, die er alle in eine grosse weisse Schüssel warf. Dann und wann rief er seine Frau, die Annes Kopf zu halten hatte, zu sich hin, zeigte ihr ein Stück Fleisch, tuschelte mit ihr, fragte sie etwas, sie zuckte mit den Schultern, kehrte zu Annes Kopf zurück, während er die Metzelei fortsetzte.[4]

The doctor, who has not administered any anesthetic at all, is unable to stop the bleeding, so he eventually tells Anne she must go to the hospital and he warns her not to tell anyone who he is. But after an hour she has stopped bleeding, Anne later recounts, " . . . und da grinste er mich an. Er sagte: 'Sie haben Schwein gehabt. Die in der Klinik sind nicht sehr freundlich, wenn ein krimineller Abort eingeliefert wird.' "

Whereas in Schallück the contemplated abortion served as the mental tripwire for the interjection and subsequent associative evaluation of a variety of related questions (murder and war, euthanasia and genocide, religion and moral values, existentialism and nihilism), in Walser, although related matters such as the abortion's illegality do enter in, the loathsome reality of the process of abortion itself overshadows all tangential arguments and questions, surely arousing supreme subliminal disgust in all but the most perverse. Hence, Walser's argument, though simpler, states even more eloquently the same case that Schallück does by making the stage for this realization not the mind of Thomas Abbt, but, by sheer realism of the narrative, the mind of the reader. In Walser whatever the logical, ethical, moral, historical, environmental, geo-

---

[4] Martin Walser, *Ehen in Phillipsburg*, p. 86f.

political or legal considerations, abortion remains for the heart and soul of human beings, even those without so much as a fragmented ethical code, a primeval form of murder.

This is made especially clear by examining the structure of Walser's entire novel, since there the same process of associative escalation as in Schallück's can be seen. Each of the four major sections of his book, for instance, culminates in the violent death of one innocent being, the first three of which are, in this order: the *feticide*, again the lowest common moral denominator, the *suicide* of a woman driven to despair by her adulterous husband, and the automobile *homicide* of a poor proletarian cyclist by yet another adulterous husband from this debauched upper crust of capitalistic Phillipsburg society, who is trying to wink suggestively at his mistress in the rear view mirror while speeding wildly through the streets in his powerful Gatsbyesque automobile. The fourth and final death, however, more horrible than all, towards which all the previous *-cides* point, and in which they culminate, is *not* caused here by the blast of a hydrogen bomb as one might have anticipated, but is more mythical in tone, a subtle artistic reenactment of the death of Christ, caused by Hans Beumann, at this point in his decline the very personification of the evil principle. In addition to the element of deicide, this culminating variation on the theme involves recapitulating overtones of homicide and suicide (the killing of Hans' own *alter ego*), which in turn harks back to the feticide and to the time Hans' mother refused to allow Hans to be aborted.

The scene of this ritualistic killing par excellence is an exclusive brothel, the Sebastian club, which, from the point of view of decor alone, is nothing less than a secularized church, externally paralleling and signifying the progressive loss of the traditional moral values discussed above. Statuary and icons of all sorts, especially of the martyred Saint Sebastian, have been taken from their churches to adorn and lend significance to this setting, into which a stranger now steps, Hermann by name, thirty-three years old, with 'several followers,' whose family name, the club's members surmise, is either Christlieb or Schäfler or Schorer, all of which, obviously, refer to his kerygmatic nature, just as popular etymology *could* make the name 'Hermann' a token of divine incarnation: *Herr* plus *Mann*. In any case the members of the club especially resent his intrusion—he has mysteriously obtained certain secret keys—because some of the club's girls have chosen to associate with his group and even follow them through the streets. Beumann, who wishes to prove his courage and win a permanent key to the club, challenges Hermann to a fight. But even as he squares off to do battle with him and looks into his dark, gentle eyes, Hans vaguely realizes he is confronting a kind of *alter ego*, a boy from the same social class, with the same proletarian background; however he does not, apparently, realize he is also confronting a Christ-figure. Hans lunges at him, they fall backwards down some stairs onto a terrace, and Hans' knee is injured—this reverse Jacob has battled with God. Hermann is merely knocked unconscious by the fall, but thanks to his careful use of ambivalent language, Walser's tableau skillfully depicts something more: a classical removal of the dead Christ from the cross, with the women bringing water and cloths to wash his body as his disciples bend over their leader trying to 'revive' him. The imagery is clear enough: Hans Beumann, at least in intent, has now become symbolically guilty of the death of God, and of all the other innocents, retracing, with his deeds, the genesis of absolute evil.

III

On the last page of Walser's novel, as if in reverse, unconscious tribute to Schallück's "wenn man aufhören könnte zu lügen," Hans Beumann gleefully discovers, "am Telefon kann man lügen lernen." Yet another six years later it is the telephone which now forms the central imagery of a novel where the topic of abortion appears for the third time. This is Heinrich Böll's *Ansichten eines Clowns* (1963). Here, though the abortion episode is shorter and less detailed, it serves nonetheless as one of the central turning points of the novel—the juncture at which the Catholic Marie gives up a kind of common-law marriage with the freethinking Protestant clown/seer Hans Schnier to marry properly an orthodox member of her own faith. Here, too, are the previously discussed elements, including the polar opposition of the individual, interior, unorthodox ethic to its traditional, exterior, orthodox counterpart. This is, in fact, the message of the entire novel, the clown being the representative of the one and the orthodox Catholics like Marie and her husband the other.

But it is the mythic dimension seen in Walser that is carried on in this book to its most subtle and at the same time most powerful conclusion. Here, in the apperceptive mind of the limping seer, which is keenly attuned to such higher significance, the angelic annunciation to Marie is nullified, the modern-day immaculate conception tainted by the decision of this postwar Virgin Mary to have an abortion. Not surprisingly, it is precisely her narrow, codified religious system which causes her to crucify grotesquely the divine child *in utero*, the most economical and, admittedly, the most hideous image to this point.

Although the mythic role of Marie's abortion is not glaringly evident to a casual reader of Böll's book, it does emerge clearly enough through the careful assembly of seemingly unrelated clues like the following: In chapter 12, at the beginning of the paragraph after the subject of Marie's abortion is first subtly revealed—she tells Hans she has had to go to the hospital with some mysterious gynecologic ailment—Hans has a vision of an 'abortive' adoration of the Magi. He sees from the hotel window "einen kleinen Jungen von links die Strasse heraufkommen . . . mit einem Gesichtsausdruck wie ich ihn auf Bildern von den Heiligen Drei Königen gesehen habe, die dem Jesuskind Weihrauch, Gold und Myrrhe hinhalten."[5] When Hans tells Marie about this boy she becomes inexplicably angry and demands concrete proof of his existence, but by this time the boy has vanished. To Hans' visionary way of thinking, however, the matter is painfully clear: Marie falls because she fails to develop an interior moral code and flees back to the supposed safety of an exterior one. When she leaves him, whom she loves, to marry someone she cannot love, even though the Pope personally approves the marriage, she commits adultery. And she becomes the symbolic murderess—at least potentially—of self, God, and all humanity by her act of abortion. Despite, or precisely because of, exterior 'thou-shalt-nots,' the interior system has failed.

The pattern to this point, it would seem, is relatively clear: In the works discussed here, abortion is the lowest common denominator and at the same time the *ne plus ultra* of killing; the murder of an embryo is evil in its most embryonic form. It is the ethical prerequisite to suicide, homicide, genocide and deicide. And it is widely found in postwar German literature because German writers happen to be, at this period in history, among the most sensitive to such germinal manifestations of evil. Among all peoples, the one which produced a Nietzsche and the death of God and by following the moral leadership of other self-proclaimed supermen subsequently came closest to inflicting total destruction upon other races and upon the whole world, is the one also most likely to produce those who think symbolically, even apocalyptically, about such topics as abortion. Among all peoples, Germans are the ones whose recent past has forced some visionaries among them to scrutinize and reevaluate most carefully all manifestations of contemporary behavior. While most of the western world in the last few years has come to tolerate abor-

---

[5] Heinrich Böll, *Ansichten eines Clowns* (Munich: DTV, 1967), p. 120f.

tions or openly to advocate them, often with the same zeal as that devoted to the *protection* of baby seals, it is our German mantics who have the freshest memory of, the fewest illusions about and the deepest fear for the extermination of earth's *most* endangered species: mankind. For them it is the human *and* the hydrogen warheads, predatory capitalism and revolutionism, chauvinistic fanaticism on sport- and battlefields, in short, man's very inhumanity to man that will destroy the earth, not the doubling, trebling or quadrupling of its peaceful population.

IV

One could, for this reason, undoubtedly list other postwar German literary examples, like *Die Ermittlung* by Peter Weiss, or Rolf Hochhuth's *Stellvertreter*, in which nazi atrocities in the concentration camps include and are symbolized by inhuman medical experiments, some involving abortions. These would certainly all serve to demonstrate the validity of the pattern.[6] One inconsistency, however, one complicating contradiction seems to have been rising. Aren't these German writers liberals, after all? Progressives, social democrats, isn't Walser even a communist? Haven't all these groups, including the SPD, supported for years all attempts to repeal or liberalize anti-abortion statutes like Paragraph 218 of the German legal code? Haven't Schallück, Böll and Walser, to name only these three, openly declared their opposition to the old law and called for its repeal? How then is one to explain this dilemma? Do these men oppose abortion in their *Dichtung* and advocate it in *Wahrheit* or have they changed their minds recently? Perhaps they simply oppose discriminatory *illegal* abortions,

---

[6] Cf. also Ilse Aichinger's "Spiegelgeschichte"; Hubert Fichte's *Die Palette;* and Ödön von Horvath's *Don Juan kommt aus dem Krieg.*

where the doctor is a quack and the knitting needles unsterile? Or has the foregoing been a complete misinterpretation of their writings? Has it forced them into a prejudicial, moralizing mold? Before unanimously deciding on the latter of these possibilities, perhaps one more prominent case should be investigated, that of Günter Grass, who in the spring of 1974 decided to give up his membership in the Catholic church in open protest of its pressure tactics in the parliamentary debates on 218. For abortions, one searches his writings almost, but not quite, in vain.[7] However, this one small early poem entitled "Familiär", from the collection *Die Vorzüge der Windhühner* (1956), seems to make up in pertinence and impact what it lacks in size:

> In unserem Museum,—wir besuchen es jeden Sonntag,—
> hat man eine neue Abteilung eröffnet.
> Unsere abgetriebenen Kinder, blasse, ernsthafte Embryos,
> sitzen dort in schlichten Gläsern
> und sorgen sich um die Zukunft ihrer Eltern.[8]

It may be that Grass has compressed into these thirty-three words the entire scope of the problem of abortion from the postwar German point of view: Expressed here, for example, is the familiar loss of traditional religious values—we now visit the museum on Sundays instead of going to church—and in the new exhibit we view our own embryonic, interior *alter egos* in an unsurpassedly exterior setting: the distanced, abstract coolness required to view one's own fetus in a glass jar

---

[7] In *Die Blechtrommel* Oskar's mother dies as a result of self-afflicted purgations she hopes will cause an abortion, even if the narrator Oskar obscures the fact by suggesting more mythic possibilities. The poem "Advent" deals with "Eltern, die überall rumstehen und vom Kinderanschaffen und Kinderabschaffen reden . . . ," and finally, in Grass' *Kopfgeburten, oder die Deutschen sterben aus* (1980), a female protagonist begins to realize that her abortion is related to the demographic demise of the Germans.
[8] Günter Grass, *Gesammelte Gedichte*, p. 61.

must be nearly absolute, providing an almost perfect, if unexpected reification of Thomas Abbt's metaphoric "drinnen ist nichts, alles ist draussen." We, the parents, then, having no interior value systems, are unable to have any feeling for the gravity of our situation. But the children, like poets and fools who always tell the truth, those pale, earnest embryos who sit there in simple glass (!) jars and frown with concern for the future of their parents, must sense somehow that the apocalyptic chain of -*cides* has begun with their death and will end with the death of mankind.

This poem, for all its compactness—it completes the trend we have seen toward tighter, more economical, symbolical expression of the problem—also goes beyond the familiar elements of the pattern to shed new light on the apparent contradictions raised above. There is no doubt, for instance, that the abortions mentioned here have been legal, clinical and sterile, since in fact, that legally clinical sterility is a major part of the problem. So the poem completely eliminates, it would seem, the possibility that all this to-do really concerns the problem of illegal abortions.

But what about the other possibilities? Two things must be conceded: one is that an author's opinion does not always necessarily coincide with the point of view, thrust or moral of the work of literature, despite the fact that he or she created the work. The phenomenon is altogether too well documented to be denied, that works of art, like the very language and imagery of a poem, often assume a mind and will of their own, compelling their 'creators' with irresistible forces of logic and consistency to write, form, compose and to act in a way altogether new to their personal natures or inclinations. In fact, it seems possible that an author must often approach his or her own completed work like everyone else, having become just another critic, 'the midwife of the idea, perhaps, but not always its father or mother.' And it has happened that where the thrust of a work has initially persuaded everyone, reading public, critic and author alike, the work itself has been subsequently neglected and the lesson subsequently forgotten, even by the artist. But even though these factors may have played a small role in producing this seeming dilemma, it is doubtful whether the problem can be totally explained in this way. Böll, Schallück, Grass and Walser are hardly that completely forgetful; these outspoken advocates of engaged literature could have hardly completely changed their minds, or have missed their own point. To understand these authors' support for the repeal of Paragraph 218, one must come full circle and reexamine the initial question, that of absolute systems of morality and their most absurd reduction: the legislation of morality. It appears that the disgust of Böll, Schallück, Walser and Grass toward abortion—given the increasing distance from these earlier works—has been eclipsed, but not necessarily rescinded, by an even more intense aversion toward the systematic, exterior, traditional, dictated morality expressed in Paragraph 218. It appears that their most recent poetic expressions of concern run in this direction, without really taking back the validity of earlier protests against abortion, and it appears that these later statements have been evoked by new, more dangerous trends.

In his *Aus dem Tagebuch einer Schnecke* (1972), for example, Father Grass lectures his sons Franz and Raoul on the dangers of an absolute moral system:

> Es könnte sein, Franz und Raoul, dass euch später, wenn ihr was sucht, der Kommunismus Hoffnung macht; er lebt davon, Hoffnung auf den kommenden, den wahren Kommunismus zu machen. Ihr könntet eines Tages, weil in Deutschland die Theorie vor die Wirklichkeit gestellt ist, in jenem totalen System, das in sich zu stimmen vorgibt und schmerzlose Übergänge verspricht, die Lösung finden wollen. (Das befriedete Dasein.) Es könnte euch Glaube hellsichtig für ein Endziel und blind für die Menschen in ihrer Gegenwart machen. (Die paar Tausend Unbelehrbaren.) Es könnte euch Unrecht als Vorleistung für die grosse, alles umfassende Gerechtigkeit billig werden. (Subjektivismus hält uns nur

auf.) Es könnte sein, dass euch das Ziel alles ist und euch die
Wünsche weniger Böhmen nichts bedeuten. (Kleinbürgerlich.) Es
ist mein Recht zu befürchten, ihr könntet euch, nachdem Zeit
verstrichen ist und weil sich Geringeres als zu schwierig erwiesen
hat, das Ziel setzen, die Befreiung der Menschheit durch den
Kommunismus (den wahren) zu erzwingen: um jeden Preis.
Ich sage: Es könnte . . .
Ich sage: Ich stünde euch dann im Wege.[9]

In the Grass poem entitled "Die neue Mystik, oder: Ein
kleiner Ausblick auf die utopischen Verhältnisse nach der
vorläufig allerletzten Kulturrevolution" (when, as the first line
reveals, " . . . unsere Fragebögen lückenhaft blieben . . ."
i.e. when internal, individual guidance systems began to fail),
the final chorus becomes an ironic panegyric to the new
medium, a clear personification of the exterior ethical source,
the moral dictator par excellence, who has usurped even the
traditional role of Holy Mother. To this new Marxist medium
we look for external answers to our internal problems:

Denn immer noch gibt die Heilige Antwort.
Um einen Tisch sitzt die Welt und holt Rat bei ihr.
Sie, die irrationale, rüstet uns ab,
sie, die telekinetische, hilft uns, das Soll zu erfüllen,
sie, die okkulte, ernährt und verwaltet uns,
nur sie, die parteiliche und unfehlbare,
sie, die gebenedeite und schmerzensreiche,
sie, die liebliche Sensitive,
füllt unsere Fragebögen,
benennt unsere Strassen,
säubert uns gründlich,
erlöst uns vom Zweifel,
nimmt uns das Kopfweh.
Fortan müssen wir nicht mehr denken,
nur noch gehorchen
und ihre Klopfzeichen auswerten.[10]

"*One* of the manifestations of evil which Germans were

---

[9] Günter Grass, *Aus dem Tagebuch einer Schnecke* (Neuwied: Luchterhand, 1972), p. 172.
[10] Günter Grass, *Gesammelte Gedichte,* p. 228f.

to learn to recognize and shun is abortion" I stated near the beginning of this chapter. Now perhaps the sentence can be completed by adding " . . . but the main form of evil is a comprehensive ethical system dictated from above, that is, from outside the individual human heart and mind, since it may lead to any or all the horrible consequences of a state of dulled individual conscience including, but not limited to: feticide, suicide, homicide, genocide and deicide." As far as Böll, Grass, Walser and Schallück are concerned, Paragraph 218 is simply the visible tip of the iceberg. Where the church or state (or crowd behavior and 'new rules' at athletic events) subverts individual moral behavior by legislating or otherwise dictating a system of rules, and the people submit themselves willingly to the rules of such authority figures, then the apocalyptic vision will be fulfilled, the museums can open new exhibits and fully expect the completely dehumanized robot/citizens to come, on Sunday or on any other day, coolly to view—not only their aborted children—but their mercy-killed cripples, the murdered bodies of their elderly, their undesirables and their Gods.

Index

Abe, Kobo, 66
Adenauer, Konrad, 25, 45
Aichinger, Ilse, 120n
Alekhine, Alexander, 78n
Antonowytsch, Michael, 71n
Arms, Robert, 67n
Arnold, Heinz Ludwig, 23n, 26n
Aronson, Elliot, 80n
Asimov, Isaac, 66, 67

Bächtold-Stäubli, Hanns, 31n
Bacon, Roger, 31n
Ball, Donald W., 80n
Bellow, Saul, 40n
Benn, Gottfried, 108
Benseler, Dr., 23, 24
Bernett, Hajo, 73n
Besterman, Theodore, 29, 31n
Blake, William, 96
Böll, Heinrich, x, 8–10 *passim*, 13, 15, 35, 57, 60, 61, 94, 95, 118, 119, 120, 123, 125
Borchert, Wolfgang, x, 3–7 *passim*, 8, 13, 15, 35, 51, 58, 82, 91, 92
Boyle, Robert H., 67n
Brautigan, Richard, 107

Brecht, Bertolt, 103, 104, 105
Broch, Hermann, 103, 105, 106
Brueghel, Jan, 16

Camus, Albert, 66
Capote, Truman, 40n
Carlyle, Thomas, 100n
Claudius, 52
Clausewitz, Carl von, 72
Coakley, Jay J., 89n, 91
Cobby, Barrie, 81
Coubertin, Pierre de, 73

Diller, Edward, 34n
Dürer, Albrecht, 16
Dürrenmatt, Friedrich, 35

Edschmid, Kasimir, 23
Eichmann, Adolf, 82, 84
Eiselen, Ernst, 71, 72n
Emrich, Wilhelm, 23
Endres, Elizabeth, ixn
Enzensberger, Hans Magnus, 23, 24

Featherston, Donald F., 66n
Fest, Joachim, 32, 33

Fichte, Hubert, 120n
Fisher, A. Craig, 67n
Fitzgerald, F. Scott, 65, 97, 98
Flaubert, Gustave, 66
Freud, Sigmund, 39n

García Marquez, Gabriel, 66
Goethe, Johann Wolfgang von, 97n
Goldstein, Jeffrey, 67n
Golombek, Harry, 76, 77n
Gorky, Maxim, 74
Görtz, Franz Joseph, 23n, 26n
Grass, Günter, x, 13–34 *passim*, 35, 59, 60, 61, 66, 95, 101, 106, 121, 123, 124, 125
Graves, Robert, 37–40 *passim*

Handrick, Paulhans, 65
Harris, H. A., 70n
Harscheidt, Michael, 34n
Hauptmann, Gerhart, 97n
Hawthorne, Nathaniel, 96
Hayes, Woody, 89
Hays, Peter, 36, 37, 48
Hemingway, Ernest, 65
Hesse, Hermann, 13n, 95
Himmler, Heinrich, 82
Hitler, Adolf, 27, 33, 72, 73, 78, 82, 98, 99, 103
Hochhuth, Rolf, 120
Hoffmann, E. T. A., 101
Höllerer, Walter, 23
Holmes, Judith, 73n
Homer, 70
Horvath, Ödön von, 120n
Huizinga, Johan, 65, 69, 70, 71, 79

Ilyin-Zhenevsky, A. F., 76

Jackson, Edward, 30n
Jahn, Friedrich Ludwig, 71, 72

Jens, Walter, 23
Jerome, 39
Johnson, William, 90

Kafka, Franz, 97n
Kaiser, Georg, 101, 102, 104
Kaiser, Joachim, 23
Kempowski, Walter, 60n
Killian, Lewis, 80
Kleist, Heinrich von, 36
Klepsch, Egon, 27n
Kollwitz, Käthe, 108
Korn, Karl, 23
Kozmina, V. P., 74n
Kuleshov, A., 75

Lawrence, D. H., 40
Lenz, Siegfried, x, 11–13 *passim*, 15, 35
Leonard, John, 65
Lindzey, Gardner, 80n
Loschütz, Gert, 23n
Loy, John, 80n
Luchterhand, Hermann & Co., 22, 23

Mailer, Norman, 65
Malamud, Bernard, 40n, 65
Malinovsky, Rodion Yakovlevich, 76
Mandelkow, Karl Robert, 101
Mann, Thomas, 32n
Martini, Fritz, 23
Marx, Karl, 102n
Marx, Leo, 96–98 *passim*, 100n
Maser, Werner, 33n
Meggysey, Dave, 87
Milgram, Stanley, 80, 82–86 *passim*
Morton, Henry W., 74, 75n
Mumford, Lewis, 95, 99, 100, 101n

Murray, H. J. R., 77n

Nettleship, M. A., 67n
Nietzsche, Friedrich, 108

Ottinger, Emil, 23

Prater, D. A., 78n

Ranke, Leopold von, 32
Richards, David John, 76n
Riordan, James, 74n
Roberts, Michael, 65, 66n, 68, 69, 75, 82n, 88n
Rosen, Edward, 30n
Rose, Pete, 66
Roth, Phillip, 65
Runfola, Ross Thomas, 81, 82

Schaap, Dick, 73n
Schallück, Paul, x, 41–52 *passim*, 55–57 *passim*, 62, 63, 93, 94, 95, 96n, 99, 100, 110–116 *passim*, 117, 120, 122, 123, 125
Schickelgruber (for Adolf Hitler), 27
Schifrin, Roy, 77
Schiller, Friedrich, 100, 101
Schilling (Oberregierungsrat), 23
Schmidt, Helmut, 64, 89
Schreck (Hitler's chauffeur), 98
Shakespeare, William, 96
Shelley, Mary W., 101n
Sipes, Richard G., 67n
Smithers, Paul, 81, 82
Smith, Michael D., 80n

Snyder, Eldon E., 67, 80, 89n
Speer, Albert, 98, 99
Spence, Lewis, 31n
Spina, Alexander de., 30n
Spreitzer, Elmer, 67, 80, 89n
Stalin, 74
Strauss, Franz Josef, 25, 26

Thompson, Stith, 31n
Toch, Hans, 80
Toller, Ernst, 36, 102, 103, 104
Tomjanovich, Rudi, 89
Turner, Ralph, 80
Twain, Mark, 96, 97

Updike, John, 65

Vogel, Hans-Jochen, 64, 65n, 89
Vogt, Joseph, 23

Walser, Martin, x, 7, 8, 13, 15, 26, 35, 59, 114–117 *passim*, 118, 120, 123, 125
Ward, Stephen D., 67, 81
Warren, Robert Penn, 40n
Wedekind, Frank, 107, 108
Weiss, Peter, 120
Wells, H. G., 66
Williams, Tennessee, 40n
Willoughby, L. A., 97n
Wolf, Friedrich, 108n

Ziesel, Kurt, 23n, 34n
Ziolkowski, Theodore, 31n
Zweig, Arnold, 108n
Zweig, Stefan, 77–79 *passim*, 108n

studia humanitatis

PUBLISHED VOLUMES

Louis Marcello La Favia, *Benvenuto Rambaldi da Imola: Dantista.* xii–188 pp. US $9.25.

John O'Connor, *Balzac's Soluble Fish.* xii–252 pp. US $14.25.

Carlos García, *La desordenada codicia*, edición crítica de Giulio Massano. xii–220 pp. US $11.50.

Everett W. Hesse, *Interpretando la Comedia.* xii–184 pp. US $10.00.

Lewis Kamm, *The Object in Zola's Rougon-Macquart.* xii–160 pp. US $9.25.

Ann Bugliani, *Women and the Feminine Principle in the Works of Paul Claudel.* xii–144 pp. US $9.25.

Charlotte Frankel Gerrard, *Montherlant and Suicide.* xvi–72 pp. US $5.00.

The Two Hesperias. Literary Studies in Honor of Joseph G. Fucilla. Edited by Americo Bugliani. xx–372 pp. US $30.00.

Jean J. Smoot, *A Comparison of Plays by John M. Synge and Federico García Lorca: The Poets and Time.* xiii–220 pp. US $13.00.

Laclos. Critical Approaches to Les Liaisons dangereuses. Ed. Lloyd R. Free. xii–300 pp. US $17.00.

Julia Conaway Bondanella, *Petrarch's Visions and their Renaissance Analogues.* xii–120 pp. US $7.00.

Vincenzo Tripodi, *Studi su Foscolo e Stern.* xii–216 pp. US $13.00.

GENARO J. PÉREZ, *Formalist Elements in the Novels of Juan Goytisolo.* xii–216 pp. US $12.50.

SARA MARIA ADLER, *Calvino: The Writer as Fablemaker.* xviii–164 pp. US $11.50.

LOPE DE VEGA, *El amor enamorado,* critical edition of John B. Wooldridge, Jr. xvi–236 pp. US $13.00.

NANCY DERSOFI, *Arcadia and the Stage: A Study of the Theater of Angelo Beolco* (called *Ruzante*). xii–180 pp. US $10.00

JOHN A. FREY, *The Aesthetics of the* ROUGON-MACQUART. xvi–356 pp. US $20.00.

CHESTER W. OBUCHOWSKI, *Mars on Trial: War as Seen by French Writers of the Twentieth Century.* xiv–320 pp. US $20.00.

JEREMY T. MEDINA, *Spanish Realism: Theory and Practice of a Concept in the Nineteenth Century.* xviii–374 pp. US $17.50.

MAUDA BREGOLI-RUSSO, *Boiardo Lirico.* viii–204 pp. US $11.00.

ROBERT H. MILLER, ed. *Sir John Harington: A Supplie or Addicion to the Catalogue of Bishops to the Yeare 1608.* xii–214 pp. US $13.50.

NICOLÁS E. ÁLVAREZ, *La obra literaria de Jorge Mañach.* vii–279 pp. US $13.00.

MARIO ASTE, *La narrativa di Luigi Pirandello: Dalle novelle al romanzo Uno, Nessuno, e Centomila.* xvi–200 pp. US $11.00.

MECHTHILD CRANSTON, *Orion Resurgent: René Char, Poet of Presence.* xxiv–376 pp. US $22.50.

FRANK A. DOMÍNGUEZ, *The Medieval Argonautica.* viii–122 pp. US $10.50.

EVERETT HESSE, *New Perspectives on Comedia Criticism.* xix–174 pp. US $14.00.

ANTHONY A. CICCONE, *The Comedy of Language: Four Farces by Molière.* xii–144 $12.00.

ANTONIO PLANELLS, *Cortázar: Metafísica y erotismo.* xvi–220 pp. US $10.00.

MARY LEE BRETZ, *La evolución novelística de Pío Baroja.* viii–476 pp. US $22.50.

Romance Literary Studies: Homage to Harvey L. Johnson, ed. Marie A. Wellington and Martha O'Nan. xxxvii–185 pp. US $15.00.

GEORGE E. MCSPADDEN, *Don Quijote and the Spanish Prologues,* volume I. vi–114 pp. US $17.00.

Studies in Honor of Gerald E. Wade, edited by Sylvia Bowman, Bruno M. Damiani, Janet W. Díaz, E. Michael Gerli, Everett Hesse, John E. Keller, Luis Leal and Russell P. Sebold. xii–244 pp. US $20.00.

LOIS ANN RUSSELL, *Robert Challe: A Utopian Voice in the Early Enlightenment.* xiii–164 pp. US $12.50.

CRAIG WALLACE BARROW, *Montage in James Joyce's* ULYSSES. xiii–218 pp. US $16.50.

MARIA ELISA CIAVARELLI, *La fuerza de la sangre en la literatura del Siglo de Oro.* xii–274 pp. US $17.00.

JUAN MARÍA COROMINAS, *Castiglione y La Araucana: Estudio de una Influencia.* viii–139 pp. US $14.00.

KENNETH BROWN, *Anastasio Pantaleón de Ribera (1600–1629) Ingenioso Miembro de la República Literaria Española.* xix–420 pp. US $18.50.

JOHN STEVEN GEARY, *Formulaic Diction in the* Poema de Fernán González *and the* Mocedades de Rodrigo. xv–180 pp. US $15.50.

HARRIET K. GREIF, *Historia de nacimientos: The Poetry of Emilio Prados.* xi–399 pp. US $18.00.

El cancionero del Bachiller Jhoan López, edición crítica de Rosalind Gabin. lvi–362 pp. US $30.00.

VICTOR STRANDBERG, *Religious Psychology in American Literature.* xi–237 pp. US $17.50.

M. AMELIA KLENKE, O.P., *Chrétien de Troyes and "Le Conte del Graal": A Study of Sources and Symbolism*.xvii–88 pp. US $11.50.

MARINA SCORDILIS BROWNLEE, *The Poetics of Literary Theory: Lope de Vega's* Novelas a Marcia Leonarda *and Their Cervantine Context.* x–182 pp. US $16.50.

NATALIE NESBITT WOODLAND, *The Satirical Edge of Truth in "The Ring and the Book."* ix–166 pp. US $17.00.

JOSEPH BARBARINO, *The Latin and Romance Intervocalic Stops: A Quantitative and Comparative Study.* xi–153 pp. US $16.50.

SANDRA FORBES GERHARD, *"Don Quixote" and the Shelton Translation: A Stylistic Analysis.* viii–166 pp. US $16.00.

EVERETT W. HESSE, *Essays on Spanish Letters of the Golden Age.* xii–208 pp. US $16.50.

VALERIE D. GREENBERG, *Literature and Sensibilities in the Weimar Era: Short Stories in the "Neue Rundschau."* Preface by Eugene H. Falk. xiii–289 pp. US $18.00.

ANDREA PERRUCCI, *Shepherds' Song (La Cantata dei Pastori)*. English version by Miriam and Nello D'Aponte. xix–80 pp. US $11.50.

MARY JO MURATORE, *The Evolution of the Cornelian Heroine*. v–153 pp. US $17.50.

FERNANDO RIELO, *Teoría del Quijote*. xix–201 pp. US $17.00.

GALEOTTO DEL CARRETTO, *Li sei contenti e La Sofonisba*, edizione e commento di Mauda Bregoli Russo. viii–256 pp. US $16.50.

BIRUTÉ CIPLIJAUSKAITÉ, *Los noventayochistas y la historia*. vii–213 pp. US $16.00.

EDITH TOEGEL, *Emily Dickinson and Annette von Droste-Hülshoff: Poets as Women*. vii–109 pp. US $11.50.

DENNIS M. KRATZ, *Mocking Epic*. xv–171 pp. US $12.50.

EVERETT W. HESSE, *Theology, Sex and the Comedia and Other Essays*. xvii–129 pp. US $14.50.

HELÍ HERNÁNDEZ, *Antecedentes italianos de la novela picaresca española: estudio lingüístico-literario*. x–155 pp. US $14.50.

ANTONY VAN BEYSTERVELDT, *Amadís, Esplanadián, Calisto: historia de un linaje adulterado*. xv–276 pp. US $24.50.

ROUBEN C. CHOLAKIAN, *The "Moi" in the Middle Distance: A Study of the Narrative Voice in Rabelais*. vii–132 pp. US $16.50.

JUAN DE MENA, *Coplas de los Siete Pecados Mortales* and First Continuation, Volume I. Edition, Study and Notes by Gladys M. Rivera. xi–212 pp. US $22.50.

JAMES DONALD FOGELQUIST, *El Amadís y el género de la historia fingida*. x–253 pp. US$21.50.

EGLA MORALES BLOUIN, *El ciervo y la fuente: mito y folklore del agua en la lírica tradicional*. x–316 pp. US $22.50.

La pícara Justina. Edición de Bruno Mario Damiani. vii–492 pp. US $33.50.

Red Flags, Black Flags: Critical Essays on the Literature of the Spanish Civil War. Ed. John Beals Romeiser. xxxiv–256 pp. US $21.50.

RAQUEL CHANG-RODRÍGUEZ, *Violencia y subversión en la prosa colonial hispanoamericana*. xv–132 pp. US $18.50.

DAVID C. LEONARD AND SARA M. PUTZELL, *Perspectives on Nineteenth-Century Heroism: Essays from the 1981 Conference of the Southeastern Studies Association*. xvi–164 pp. US $20.00.

La Discontenta and La Pythia, edition with introduction and notes by Nicholas A. De Mara. vii–214 pp. US $17.00.

CALDERÓN DE LA BARCA, The Prodigal Magician, translated and edited by Bruce W. Wardropper. vii–250 pp. US $20.00.

JOHN R. BURT, Selected Themes and Icons from Medieval Spanish Literature: Of Beards, Shoes, Cucumbers and Leprosy. xi–111 pp. US $16.50.

ALAN FRANK KEELE, The Apocalyptic Vision: A Thematic Exploration of Postwar German Literature. vii–130 pp. US $19.00.

FORTHCOMING PUBLICATIONS

HELMUT HATZFELD, Essais sur la littérature flamboyante.

NANCY D'ANTUONO, Boccaccio's novelle in Lope's theatre.

Novelistas femeninas de la postguerra española, ed. Janet W. Díaz.

PERO LÓPEZ DE AYALA, Crónica del Rey Don Pedro I, edición crítica de Heanon y Constance Wilkins.

ALBERT H. LE MAY, The Experimental Verse Theater of Valle-Inclán.

ALONSO ORTIZ, Diálogo sobre la educación del Príncipe Don Juan, hijo de los Reyes Católicos. Introducción y versión de Giovanni Maria Bertini.

DARLENE J. SADLIER, Cecília Meireles: Imagery in "Mar Absoluto."

ARIÉ SERPER, Huon de Saint-Quentin: Poète satirique et lyrique. Etude historique et édition de textes.

BEVERLY WEST, Epic, Folk, and Christian Traditions in the "Poema de Fernán González."

ROBERT COOGAN, Babylon on the Rhone: A Translation of Letters of Dante, Petrarch, and Catherine of Siena on the Avignon Papacy.

ROBERT A. DETWEILER AND SARA M. PUTZELL-KORAB, eds. Crisis in the Humanities.

LAWRENCE H. KLIBBE, Lorca's "Impresiones y paisajes": The Young Artist.

OHIO UNIVERSITY LIBRARY

Please return this book as soon as you have finished with it. In order to avoid a

4